THE FUTURE OF INDIAN POLITICS

THE FUTURE OF INDIAN POLITICS

By M. N. Roy

GYAN

Published by

Gyan Publishing House
5, Ansari Road
Daryaganj, New Delhi-110002
Phone: 011-47034999, 9811692060
E-mail: books@gyanbooks.com

Distribution Network
gyanbooks.com
India, USA, Canada, UK, Australia

ISBN: 978-93-6208-666-2 (PB)
First Published, 1929

2nd Impression 2024

Printed at: Gyan Press, Delhi.

THE FUTURE OF INDIAN POLITICS
Author: M. N. ROY

THE FUTURE OF INDIAN POLITICS

THE FUTURE OF INDIAN POLITICS

By M. N. ROY

CONTENTS

PART I. THE ECONOMICS OF COMPROMISE

PART II. THE POLITICS OF COMPROMISE

PART III. A REAL NATIONALIST MOVEMENT

PREFACE

IN this book the historic necessity for a People's Party in India is dealt with. The question of the party of the proletariat is purposely left out. The role of the proletariat in the struggle for national freedom and democratisation of the country is defined only in broad outlines. Political organisation of the proletariat, its structure and programme, do not enter into the purview of the book. The proletariat is considered as a component part of the Nationalist forces. By the omission of the question, the importance of the party of the proletariat is not in the least minimised. Neither is the People's Party meant to be a substitute for the party of the proletariat. The object of this book is to show a way to the revolutionary Nationalist forces; to point out the causes of the decline of bourgeois Nationalism; to expose the tendency of compromise underneath the verbal radicalism of the upper middle class; to indicate the historic necessity for the fight for freedom; and to enunciate in general the programme and organisational form the fight is bound to assume in its coming phases. Although the proletariat is destined to act as the lever of the struggle for national liberation, there are other social classes immensely more numerous than the proletariat whose importance in the fight for democratic national freedom cannot be minimised. The future of Indian politics will still be dominated by the interests of these classes—intellectuals, artisans, small traders and peasantry. How to organise these forces of national revolution in a democratic party is the immediate problem before the Indian revolutionaries. The proletariat being the revolutionary vanguard must help to solve this problem. The hegemony of the proletariat in the struggle for national freedom should be so exercised as not to circumscribe, but to intensify the fullest display of the energy of the forces of national revolution. This will be done through the People's Party as demonstrated in the following pages.

THE AUTHOR.

THE FUTURE OF INDIAN POLITICS

PART I

THE ECONOMICS OF COMPROMISE

Chapter I. The Social Basis of Imperialism

Bourgeois Nationalism in India has ended in a complete compromise with imperialism, as was predicted years ago by those who judged the situation with Marxian realism. Side by side with national antagonism, class antagonism developed during the post-war period of the Indian Nationalist movement. Gradually the latter antagonism became predominant over the former. The process of class differentiation inside the Nationalist ranks caused constant political regrouping. The predominating tendency was toward the formation of a bourgeois bloc of constitutional opposition. Imperialism helped this tendency very cleverly and successfully with the policy of "Economic Concession and Political Repression"—economic concession to Indian capitalism to draw the Nationalist bourgeoisie closer to the British Government, thus isolating the middle class Nationalists, whose comparatively radical political activities were dealt with by the firm hand of repressive laws. The move to the Right—towards compromise with imperialism—was marked by two very distinct stages : first, divorce of the bourgeois Nationalist movement from the most revolutionary social forces—workers and peasants ; second, the schism between the big bourgeoisie and the petty bourgeoisie. The first was accomplished in 1923 when the revolutionary programme of mass passive resistance to imperialist autocracy was abandoned in favour of constitutional parliamentary obstruction. The organisation of the Swaraj Party marked the separation of the Nationalist movement from revolutionary mass action.

By the end of 1925 the schism between the big bourgeoisie and the petty bourgeoisie became wide enough to split the Swaraj Party, which for two years had served the purpose of a bridge between the constitutionalism of the big bourgeoisie and the revolutionary inclinations of the petty bourgeoisie.*

The split in the Swaraj Party means the burning of that bridge. The big bourgeoisie have decided

---

* Since this was written, the defection of the Mahratta Responsivists has culminated in a complete split of the Swaraj Party on the lines of class interests of the big bourgeoisie and of the lower middle class.

to shake off the encumbrance of the petty bourgeois political vagaries, notwithstanding the fact that the latter have served their purpose. The split in the Swaraj Party removes the last obstacle to a happy compromise between the Indian bourgeoisie and British imperialism, of course under the hegemony of the latter.

The desire for this compromise is not one-sided. British imperialism is very desirous of stabilising the economical and political situation in India. It has long been recognised by far-seeing imperialist statesmen that a country like India cannot be kept long in subjugation without the active and willing support of an influential section of the native population. In other words, imperialism must have a social basis in India. Until the earlier years of the twentieth century, British imperialism in India relied upon two native factors: one positive, the other negative. The first was the loyalty of the reactionary landed aristocracy which had been partly created and partly bolstered up by the British conquerors. The second was the passivity of the masses. Relying on these two factors, British imperialism could afford to ignore the feeble demands of the rising bourgeoisie and the revolutionary dissatisfaction growing among the petty intellectuals. Besides, until the World War, the economics of imperialism demanded that India (as well as other colonial countries) should be held in a state of industrial backwardness in order to supply a market and raw materials for the metropolitan industries. Consequently the relation between imperialism and the colonial bourgeoisie was that of antagonism. This antagonism found its expression in the Nationalist movement. But there was another economic consideration which made the Nationalism of the Indian bourgeoisie weak and compromising even in those days. Owing to the forced industrial backwardness of the country, the Indian bourgeoisie were mostly engaged in distributing trade which was dependent on British imperialism both politically and economically. Politically, because security and expansion of trade required a stable government and order in the country, conditions which had been fulfilled by the British. Economically, because both the export and import trade being practically a British monopoly, the Indians engaged in it were economic vassals of imperialism. The Nationalist movement inspired and headed by such a weak social class did not disturb imperialism. The terrorist secret societies, through which the growing discontent of the unemployed and unemployable petty intellectuals was spasmodically expressed, could be dealt with successfully by brutal repression.

The situation remained more or less like this till the eve of the World War. Soon after the outbreak of the world conflagration, it became evident that British domination in India could no longer be maintained on the old narrow social basis. The social basis of British rule could be widened and deepened only by drawing at least the upper strata of the Nationalist bourgeoisie within the economic orbit of imperialism. This necessitated a change in the economic policy of imperialism. Still another factor contributed to that change, and precipitated it. The exigencies of war obliged Britain to relax her grip on the economic life of India.

Thus began the new era when imperialist interests were so changed as to render an agreement with the Indian bourgeoisie desirable and profitable.

Chapter II. Dividing the Spoils

All along, the grievance of the Indian bourgeoisie had been that the British Government impeded the industrial development of India. The two main planks of the Nationalist platform were fiscal autonomy and administrative reforms. The demand for fiscal autonomy grew energetic in proportion to the accumulation of capital in the hands of the Indian bourgeoisie. The phenomenal growth of British trade with India had unavoidably caused a proportionate accumulation of capital in the hands of the Indian bourgeoisie. The phenomenal growth of British trade with India had unavoidably caused a proportionate accumulation of capital in the hands of the Indian mercantile class connected with that prosperous trade. The following table shows the growth of India's foreign trade in the 40 years preceding the World War which caused a revolution in Britain's economic relations with India:

Foreign Trade
(In millions of rupees.)

Quinquennial Average	Export	Import	Excess Export
1874-79 ...	630	380	250
1879-84 ...	790	590	200
1884-80 ...	880	610	270
1889-94 ...	1,040	710	330
1894-99 ...	1,070	740	330
1899-04 ...	1,220	850	370
1904-09 ...	1,440	1,030	410
Annual			
1909-10 ...	1,880	1,220	660
1910-11 ...	2,090	1,330	760
1911-12 ...	2,280	1,440	840
1912-13 ...	2,460	1,660	800
1913-14 ...	2,490	1,910	580

It will be noticed that the characteristic of this large volume of trade has always been a considerable excess of export over import. In countries in a normal economic (capitalist) condition, such a continual favourable balance of trade indicates a state of "national prosperity." But in India it was not the case. "National wealth" does not belong to the nation. It is the property of that social class which controls the economic life of the nation. The economic life of India not being controlled by the native bourgeoisie, the accumulated wealth produced by the people (workers and peasants) did not contribute to the capitalist development of the country.

The portion of the commodities exported, that was not covered by imports, did not go to create credit in favour of India. The surplus Indian export represented mostly the tribute to imperialism; nevertheless a part was appropriated by the native trading bourgeoisie in a manner to be explained presently.

Even now nearly 70 per cent. of India's exports are raw materials and foodstuff. During the period covered by the above table the proportion was still greater. By far the largest portion of the raw materials exported were produced by the small peasantry, there being very little large-scale farming in India, except the tea plantations. The unpaid excess export, therefore, indicated a terrible exploitation of the peasantry. Imports were and still are mostly manufactured goods. The comparative smallness of their volume shows the corresponding limitedness of the buying capacity of the Indian masses. The latter produced and were obliged to give up much more than they could get in return. The proceeds of the exploitation of the Indian peasantry, reflected in the trade balance in favour of India, was divided between British imperialism and Indian traders. A portion of the surplus exports was paid up by the import of gold and silver which was mostly absorbed by the upper classes of Indian society. The remaining portion went to the account of liquidating Indian obligations to England for the benefit of British rule.

The following table shows how the value of excess export was divided up till the war:

DIVISION OF EXCESS EXPORT VALUE.

(In millions of rupees.)

QUINQUENNIAL AVERAGE		EXCESS EXPORT	TREASURE IMPORTED*	TO LIQUIDATE OBLIGATIONS†
1874-79	...	250	100	150
1879-84	...	200	120	80
1884-89	...	270	130	140
1889-94	...	330	140	190
1894-99	...	330	80	250
1899-04	...	370	140	230
1904-09	...	410	220	190
ANNUAL				
1909-10	...	660	310	350
1910-11	...	760	320	440
1911-12	...	840	490	350
1912-13	...	800	510	290
1913-14	...	580	370	210

These tables are compiled from the figures in the Government Statistical Abstract. Round numbers approximating the exact value are used.

* The item treasure is practically all covered by gold and silver bullion, apart from that imported by the Government for coinage.

† India's obligations in Britain consist of pensions for the retired English civil and military officials, payment for the Government stores and supplies, and interest and sinking fund for the debts floated in the English market on behalf of the Government of India. India's public debt in Britain amounts to about 450 millions sterling, the annual recurring charges for interest and sinking fund being about 20 million sterling at present.

Thus the portion of the surplus value extracted from the Indian masses only through the unpaid amount of raw produce exported, during the period 1874-1914, in terms of money amounted to 14,440 million rupees, of which 6,650 million fell to the share of the Indian bourgeoisie. This wealth could not be converted into capital sufficiently profitably by investment in land and trade—two main avenues of exploitation open to the Indian bourgeoisie. The search for a more lucrative industrial outlet became ever more persistent and crystallised in the Nationalist demand for protection to native industry and fiscal autonomy. Nationalist economists complained bitterly against the "drain" of wealth from India, because the major portion of the surplus value produced by the masses of the population was misappropriated by foreign capitalists. According to the theory of bourgeois economics, the entire booty belonged legitimately to the native possessing classes. In that case, it would represent "national wealth" indicating prosperity of the nation, although its source just the same would be the exploitation of the producing classes. The complaint was not against the system that took away from the peasantry and other producing classes 1,444 crores of rupees in 40 years without giving anything in return. The complaint was that the entire or major part of the sum did not go into the pockets of the native bourgeoisie, and that what did fall to the share of the native bourgeoisie might be more profitably invested. Development of Indian capitalism was obstructed in the interest of British imperialism.

The programme of Nationalism as expressed by the National Congress was not based upon the irreconcilable antagonism between the foreign exploiter and the robbed Indian masses. It represented a feeble protest against the "unfair" distribution of the booty. It is remarkable—and therein lay the germ of subsequent compromise with imperialism—that the political plank of the Nationalist platform was not half as strong as the economic one of fiscal autonomy.

What is meant by fiscal autonomy? It means that India should be autonomous (of Britain) in her financial and trade operations. It is evident that the autonomy in financial and commercial spheres cannot be effective without a simultaneous political autonomy. So long as Britain remains the dominating political force—the State power—in India, she will not permit the Indian bourgeoisie to readjust the financial and trade relations in a way harmful to British interest. But significantly enough, the Nationalism of the Indian bourgeoisie never demanded political freedom—it does not do so even now.

By fiscal autonomy the Indian bourgeoisie meant a wider latitude to exploit Indian labour by converting their accumulated wealth into industrial capital. However, in course of time, they realised the impossibility of winning even that much economic freedom without some political power. In 1926, as condition for India's full support to Britain in carrying on the war to victory, the Nationalist bourgeoisie demanded self-government (within the Empire) and an immediate grant of fiscal autonomy. Imperialism could no longer remain indifferent to that demand made in a very critical moment. The first step towards agreement was taken, to be followed by others in quick succession.

CHAPTER III. THE NEW ECONOMIC POLICY OF IMPERIALISM

THE demands of the Indian bourgeoisie coincided and even had been preceded by additional and unexpected events giving rise among the imperialist statesmen to a tendency towards an agreement with the Indian bourgeoisie even before the latter definitely formulated their attitude in 1916. The then Viceroy, Lord Hardinge, in a despatch to the Secretary of State for India, in the latter part of 1915, had recommended the policy of fostering the industrial growth of India. He said:

> "It is becoming increasingly clear that a definite and self-conscious policy of improving the industrial capabilities of India will have to be pursued after the war, unless she is to become more and more a dumping ground for the manufactures of other nations. . . The attitude of the Indian public towards this important question is unanimous, and cannot be left out of account. . . . After the war, India will consider herself entitled to demand the utmost help which her government can afford to enable her to take her place, so far as circumstances permit, as a manufacturing country." (Lord Hardinge's despatch to the Secretary for India, in 1915.)

Acting on this recommendation of the Viceroy and in order to meet the demands of the Nationalist bourgeoisie, the British Government set up the Indian Industrial Commission "to examine and report upon the possibilities of further industrial development in India." A Nationalist leader and three foremost Indian capitalists sat on the Commission with representatives of imperialism. After two years of exhaustive investigation into the sources of capital, raw material, market and labour, the Commission recommended among other subsidiary things:

1. That in future the Government must play an active part in the industrial development of the country.
2. That India produces all the raw materials necessary for the requirements of a modern community, but is unable to manufacture many of the articles and materials essential alike in times of peace and war. Therefore, it is vital for the Government to ensure the establshment in India of those industries whose absence exposes us to grave danger in the event of war.
3. That modern methods should be introduced in agriculture so that labour now wastefully employed would be set free for industries.
4. That the policy of "laissez faire" in industrial affairs, to which the Government clung so long, should be abandoned.
5. That the establishment of Industrial Banks should be encouraged by means of Government financing, if necessary.
6. That the necessity for securing the economic safety of the country, and the inability of the people to secure it without the co-operation of the Government, are apparent. Therefore, the Government must adopt a policy of energetic intervention in industrial affairs.

While the Commission was still carrying on its investigation, practical effect was given to the recommendations that it made subsequently. In 1917 the Indian Munitions Board was created "to develop Indian resources to meet the necessities of war and the situation created by the war." The (English) chairman of the Industrial Commission, who had always been an advocate of the point of view that industrial development of India would strengthen the basis of imperialism, became the head of that newly created State organ which gave a tremendous impetus to Indian industry. The Munitions Board worked on the following lines:

1. Direct purchase in India of articles and materials of all kinds needed for the army, the civil departments and railways.
2. The diversion of all orders for articles and materials from the United Kingdom and elsewhere to the manufacturers in India.
3. The giving of assistance to individuals and firms in order to stabilise new industries or develop old ones.

The result was reflected in the increased share of manufactured articles in export trade from 24 per cent. to 31 per cent., reached in two years. Moreover, orders for large transport and military supplies were placed with Indian manufacturers who were given State aid to fulfil the orders. The growth of the Tata Iron and Steel Company is indicative of the situation in general.

THE TATA IRON AND STEEL PRODUCTION
(*In tons.*)

YEAR		PIG IRON	STEEL	STEEL RAILS
1915	...	154,509	66,603	45,639
1917	...	167,870	114,027	72,670
1918	...	198,064	130,043	71,096
1919	...	232,368	134,061	70,969

The net profit was as follows:

1915	...	2,805,000	rupees.
1916	...	5,103,000	,,
1917	...	7,927,500	,,
1918	...	7,900,000	,,

The next step towards agreement was the scheme of constitutional reforms prepared jointly by the Secretary of State for India, Montague, and the Viceroy, Lord Chelmsford. They proposed to give the Indian bourgeoisie and higher professional classes a share in the legislative and administrative authority of the country. The main features of the Reforms were: (1) modification of the control of the Indian Government by the British Parliament; (2) creation of central and provincial legislatures with an elected majority; (3) extension of the franchise to include the entire bourgeoisie and the upper strata of the petty bourgeoisie; (4) increase of the number of Indian members of the Viceroy's Executive Council (and appointment of Indian Ministers to the Provincial Governors in addition to Executive Councillors, both English and Indian); (5) transfer of local self-government to the Indians; (6) opening of the higher positions in civil services to Indians, etc., etc.

These political reforms (essentially very inadequate), together with the recognition of the right of Indian capital, fully satisfied the upper strata of the Indian bourgeoisie. Three years after the demand for full self-government (within the Empire) had been put forward by the united Nationalist Movement, the Moderate Party, representing the big industrialist and commercial classes, accepted in 1919 the very inadequate measure of self-government granted by the Government of India Act.

Economic concessions made under the pressure of war exigencies satisfied them. The recommendations of the Industrial Commission and the steps taken for their fulfilment meant to the big bourgeoisie, represented by the Moderate Party, more than the reforms granted by the Government of India Act. The upper strata of the bourgeoisie not only broke away from the National Congress, but fully co-operated with the Government to suppress the post-war revolutionary movement.

On the economic aspect, the Montagu-Chelmsford Scheme of Constitutional Reform expressed the following opinion:

> "As the desirability of industrial expansion became clearer, the Government of India fully shared the desire of the Indian leaders to secure the economic advantages that would follow the local manufacture of raw products. English theories as to the appropriate limits of the State's activity are inapplicable to India. We believe that this is true in case of industries, and that if the resources of the country are to be developed, the Government must take action."

It is to be noted that the concessions made were not forced by the demand of the Indian bourgeoisie alone. Two other factors of very great importance asserted themselves on the situation. They were (1) exigencies of the war, and (2) necessity of widening the social basis of imperialism. Still another factor came into play subsequently. That was the crisis of world capitalism caused by the war.

Towards the close of the world war, the negative factor—passivity of the masses—upon which British rule in India had mainly relied, almost disappeared. In spite of the maturing rapprochement between imperialism and the Nationalist bourgeoisie, the country was in a state of revolt. The necessity of widening and deepening the social basis of British rule in India by winning over the native bourgeoisie became imperative. The Reform Act of 1919 was passed by the British Parliament to meet the situation. But the first great revolutionary expression of Indian Nationalism could not be altogether suffocated by an Act of Parliament. A few years of disturbances were to follow. The revolutionary upheaval of 1919-21, however, did not hinder the process of agreement. On the contrary, the fear of revolution drove the Indian bourgeoisie into the arms of capitalism.

The appearance of tremendous revolutionary forces on the scene encouraged the petty bourgeoisie, whose position would be scarcely improved by the reforms, to oppose the reforms. Even a section of the bourgeoisie joined that opposition. But the new imperialist policy of steady economic concession to the Indian bourgeoisie, in course of time, knocked the bottom out of the opposition which took the form of boycott of the reformed legislatures. It may once more be emphasised that the policy of concession was forced upon imperialism by two considerations entirely independent of the demand of the Indian bourgeoisie. They were (1) to enlist the services of the Nationalist bourgeoisie in the attempt to suppress the revolutionary uprising of the Indian masses for freedom, and (2) to overcome the post-war crisis of capitalism by creating new markets and tapping the sources of cheap labour.

As a further encouragement to the process of Indian industrialisation, in December, 1919, the

Government moved a resolution in the Legislative Assembly, appointing a commission to give practical shape to the recommendations of the Indian Industrial Commission. The Resolution says:

> "The most obvious and direct form of assistance which the Government can give to the industries of the country is by the purchase of supplies required for the public services so far as possible in the country itself."

This measure to advance the interests of native capitalism was taken immediately after the most powerful section of the Indian bourgeoisie had broken away from the Nationalist movement. It was obviously intended to show that it paid to co-operate with imperialism even on the basis of very inadequate political reforms. Besides, British capital invested or about to be invested in India, not as previously, but for building manufacturing industries, was influencing the economic policy of imperialism.

Referring to the cause and consequences of the establishment of the Indian Stores Department, the British Trade Commission in India wrote in 1920:

> "In the first place, both the Indian and also the non-official European members of the Legislature are determined that, in future, all purchases of stores for Government requirements shall be made in India and that all tenders shall be called for in India and in rupees. These claims have been met by the Government of India to some extent. The revised Store Rules permit the newly organised Indian Stores Department at Delhi /Simla to purchase almost unlimited quan-

> tities from stocks held in India or in the course of shipment. They also sanction purchases of machinery and plant from the Indian branches of British manufacturers or from their technical agents. There seems to be little doubt that the new Indian Stores Department will rapidly increase in importance and that the centre of purchasing influence, so far as important stores are concerned, will be transferred from London to India."

Already in 1918, the Government had declared they would place an order for 3,000 railway wagons with Indian manufacturers annually for ten years, provided that the prices were not higher than the prices at which wagons could be imported from other countries. A contract was made with the Tata Company for the supply of 10,000 tons of steel plates annually for a period of ten years. The budget of 1922-23 allotted 1,500,000,000 rupees for the rehabilitation of the railways. On the motion of Sir Vithaldas Thakersey, a leading Indian industrialist and financier, the Legislative Assembly passed a resolution appointing a committee to investigate "what steps should be taken by the Government of India to encourage the establishment of the necessary industries so that as large an amount as possible of the railway rehabilitation allotment be spent in India."

Chapter IV. India adopts Protection

In its report the Railway Committee cited instances of the failure of Indian manufacturers to compete successfully with the manufacturers of other countries. Consequently the opinion of the Committee was "that industries newly started in India for the manufacture of railway materials of a fabricated character cannot, in the initial stage, compete *without assistance* against established industries abroad." As a logical consequence of this admission, the Legislative Assembly passed a Bill in June, 1924, granting bounty on the manufacture of railway wagons in India until the year 1929.

All these measures were heading towards Protectionism—the *summum bonum* of Indian Nationalist demand. To the dissatisfaction of the Indian bourgeoisie, the Industrial Commission of 1916 had been precluded from touching the tariff question. Naturally, British imperialism had been very reluctant to equip the Indian bourgeoisie with a weapon that could eventually be turned against it. But events were moving fast. The decision to purchase railway material, structural steel, etc., manufactured in India when the amount manufactured could obviously not supply the demand, was an invitation for British capital to build industries in India. The concession to the Indian bourgeoisie was incidental. The process of accumulation of capital in the industries in Britain was on the decline; should British capital not find other sources of investment which could lead to accumulation setting off the decline at home, the post-war crisis of British imperialism would be decidedly fatal. Further, the Indian market was rapidly ceasing to be a British monopoly. It was invaded from all sides—United States, Japan, Germany and Belgium taking the lead. The following tables show the situation as regards the iron and steel trade:

STEEL IMPORTS

From	1914	1922	
Britain	59.8%	45.7%	of total import.
Belgium	17.0%	30.7%	,, ,, ,,
U.S.A.	2.2%	13.7%	,, ,, ,,

Even Germany, which had been totally eliminated from the Indian market up till 1920, recovered her position by 1922 to the extent of 12.1 per cent. of the total import.

IMPORTS OF IRON BARS AND CHANNELS

(*In tons.*)

		1920	1922
Britain	...	77,726	17,616
Germany	...	9,743	38,404
Belgium	...	39,580	113,116

The textile market, which had absorbed over 30 per cent. of British export to India, was also seriously cut into by Japan. The following figures illustrate the situation:

POUNDS OF YARN IMPORTED

		Britain	Japan
1922-23	...	31,018,372	26,546,905
1923-24	...	24,789,923	20,430,025
1924-25	...	20,759,078	32,324,773

In the first quarter of 1925, Japanese import was 16,160,285 pounds as against 4,861,775 pounds from England. As regards woven goods, particularly of the finer varieties, Lancashire was still resisting the competition. But over 60 per cent. of India's textile demands consist of cheap rough stuff, owing to the low standard of living of the people. Ever-increasing quantities of yarn of the lower counts, imported from Japan, would be woven in the Indian mills and drive the Lancashire cloth out of the Indian market. The consideration of this eventuality induced the Lancashire millowners, just recently, to come to an agreement with the Indian manufacturers by acquiescing in the abolition of the Excise Duty on the Indian cotton industry.

The greatest portion of the 1,500,000,000 rupees allotted (in 1921) for the rehabilitation of railways was spent in England but in the teeth of persistent Indian demand that supplies for Indian railways should be bought in the cheapest market. Eventually Indian orders would go to other countries by the sheer law of competition (the basic principle of capitalist economy), unless Britain permitted India herself to supply them.

British manufacturers were being dislodged approximately at the corresponding rate from other Eastern markets. To manufacture in India was the only possible way out of the impasse. Cheap labour and raw materials and great saving on the cost of transport taken together would enable the British capitalists not only to hold their own in the Eastern market; the enormous profit made might also enable them to tide over the industrial crisis at home.

Soon after the conclusion of the war, a number of iron and steel manufacturing companies were registered in India, all connected with British firms. The principal ones were:

1. Indian Iron and Steel Company, Ltd.; Capital Rs. 5,000,000. Registered in 1918.

Projected production 180,000 tons of pig iron a year. Promoted by Burn and Co., a British engineering and shipbuilding firm in India.

2. The United Steel Corporation of Asia, Ltd., capital, Rs. 150,000,000. Registered in 1921. Projected annual production 300,000 tons of pig iron and 200,000 tons finished steel to be increased in a few years to 700,000 and 450,000 tons respectively. Promoted by Cammel, Laird and Co., of Sheffield.
3. The Peninsula Locomotive Co. Capital Rs. 6,000,000, held partly by Kerr, Stuart and Co., of Stoke-on-Trent, and partly by Indian capitalists. Will be able to produce 299 locomotives a year to begin with.

The lead given by these firms was sure to be followed by others. (It has been proved to be so by subsequent events.) Thus, tariff walls raised by the Indian Government would no longer operate against British interests. They would protect the Indian key industry largely promoted and owned by British capital, with native capital participating.

There was another reason which obliged British imperialism to accede to the Indian Nationalist demand for protection by a high tariff. This was a negation of the traditional policy on which British trade relations with India had always been determined. In the interest of the home manufacturers Britain imposed upon India the policy of Free Trade. In the case of India, Free Trade means free exploitation by British imperialism. The British manufacturers would not tolerate the least obstacle to be placed on the free import of their commodities to India.

Financial difficulties in the post-war years had

obliged the Indian Government to raise import duties to a height which, for practical purposes, had protectionist effects. From an average 3 per cent. ad valorem levied before the war for revenue purposes, the import duties had been raised from 11 to 15 per cent. Judged from this side, what remained to be done was to call the spade a spade—come out officially in favour of protection for India and thus satisfy the traditional demand of the Nationalist bourgeoisie.

In the beginning of 1921 the following resolution, moved by Lallubhai Samaldas (an Indian merchant and financier) was passed by the Legislative Assembly:

> "This Council recommends to the Governor-General in Council that His Majesty's Government be addressed through the Secretary of State with a prayer that the Government of India be granted full fiscal autonomy subject to the provisions of the Government of India Act."

Immediately after this resolution had been passed the Secretary of State for India in replying to a deputation from Lancashire (which had all along been the sturdy opponent to India's fiscal freedom) declared the decision:

> "To give to the Government of India the right to consider the interests of India first, just as we, without any complaint from any other parts of the Empire, and the other parts of the Empire without any complaint from us, have always chosen the tariff arrangements which they think best fitted for their needs, thinking of their own citizens first."

This speech was followed by a despatch, dated 30th June, 1921, to the Government of India, announcing the decision of the British Government to accept the principle of fiscal autonomy.

In October, 1921, was appointed a Fiscal Commission to examine the question of a tariff, under the Presidency of Sir Ibrahim Rahimtoolla—a great Bombay millowner. Out of the eleven members of the Commission, seven were Indians, all prominent in industrial, commercial and Nationalist political fields. One unprecedented feature of the Commission was that it had only one English official on it. The divergence between the interests of British and Indian capital had been so reduced that mutual confidence and joint action was possible.

The Fiscal Commission submitted its report at the end of the next year. Basing itself on the conclusions "that the industrial development of India has not been commensurate with the size of the country, its population and its natural resources, and that a considerable development of Indian industries would be very much to the advantage of the country as a whole," the Commission recommended, among other things:

1. That the Government of India adopt a policy of Protection with discrimination.
2. That a permanent Tariff Board be set up to consider the claims of particular industries for protection.
3. That raw materials and machinery be admitted free of duty.
4. That the Excise Duty on the Indian cotton industry be removed.
5. That no obstacle be raised to the free inflow

of foreign capital, but that Government monopolies or concessions be granted only to companies incorporated and registered in India with rupee capital, and with Indians on their directorates.

Five Indian members of the Commission (the President himself included among them) did not consider the verdict of the Commission wide enough and supplemented the General Report with a minute of dissent. The essence of their point of view will be interesting and useful to note, since it represents the demand of the most radical section of the Indian bourgeoisie. The dissenting minority wrote:

1. There should be an unqualified pronouncement that the fiscal policy best suited to India is *Protection*.
2. It is a mere commonplace to say that a rich India is a tower of strength to the Empire, while an economically weak India is a source of weakness. . . India would have been of far greater help to England during the war if the policy of protection had been adopted at least a generation ago. . . This (revision of the tariff policy) would have been to her great advantage and would have been beneficial to the Empire. . . .

   India, inhabited by a fifth of the human race, can be of tremendous value, economic and political, both to herself and to the Empire, if development proceeds on lines best suited to her conditions.

On the question of inflow of foreign capital, the minority appeared to differ from the view expressed in the general report. But this is what they said:

"We are unanimous in thinking that in

> the interest not only of the consumer, but of the economic advancement of the country, it is essentially necessary that industrialisation should proceed at a rapid pace. . . . We will, therefore, state at once, that we would raise no objection to foreign capital in India obtaining the benefit of protective policy, provided suitable conditions are laid down to safeguard the essential interests of India."

The conditions recommended by the minority, however, are the same as stated in the general report, namely: incorporation of companies in India with rupee capital and proportionate Indian directors.

In February, 1923, the Government of India declared the acceptance of the principle of discriminating protection recommended by the Fiscal Commission as a whole. The Government resolution unanimously adopted by the Legislative Assembly accepted "in principle the proposition that the fiscal policy of the Government of India may legitimately be directed towards fostering the development of industries in India."

A few months later, acting upon the recommendations of the Fiscal Commission, the Government appointed the Tariff Board consisting of three members, two of whom were Indians. Thus an agreement was reached between the Indian bourgeoisie and British imperialism on the vital question of economic antagonism. Without vitally injuring imperialist monopoly, considerable satisfaction was given to Indian capitalism at the expense of the masses.

The Tariff Board began, of course, with the Iron and Steel industry. The Tatas immediately came forward with the demand for a 33.5 per cent. duty on imported steel manufactures. On the recommendation of the Tariff Board, the Government in May, 1924 brought before the Legislative Assembly the Steel Industry (Protection) Bill which set up a tariff varying from 20 to 25 per cent. on fabricated iron and steel entering the country, and a large bounty on the production in India of railway wagons. The Bill authorised the Government to raise the duty in case one or more of the dutiable articles would be found to be imported into India at such a price as would be likely to render ineffective the protection intended. The Bill passed the Legislative Assembly with very little opposition. The Swaraj Party broke its vow of obstruction and voted with the Government.

The effect of protection on the Indian iron and steel industry can be judged from the following estimated growth in the production of the Tata concern behind a tariff wall. Total production in 1923 was 121,000 tons. It will increase to 250,000 335,000 and 390,000 tons in the three succeeding years.

Hardly a year after the passage of the Protection Act, the Tatas declared that the duties did not give them enough protection and demanded their increase. The Government, with the sanction of the Assembly, granted the demand not by additional duty, but by a substantial bounty on production to guarantee a fixed margin of profit.

The Tariff Board then recommended protection for the paper and cement industries and is at present considering the claims of the coal mining industry. Since the industries, whose claims are to be investigated, are suggested by the Government, the protection for these industries is a foregone conclusion.

Chapter V. The Cotton Excise and Foreign Trade

The climax of the policy, which has transformed the economic relation between the Indian bourgeoisie and British imperialism from antagonism to co-operation, was abolition of the 3.5% Excise Duty; there has been a duty of 11% on the cotton goods imported, which duty remains in force. One of the outstanding Nationalist grievances has always been "the strangling of India's premier industry in the interest of Lancashire." The phenomenal growth of the Indian cotton industry does not justify this grievance. The industry, with an aggregate capital of Rs. 300,000,000 (in round numbers) made a total clear profit of Rs.350,000,000 in the period of three years, 1919-1921. Even when in Sept. 1925, the workers (150,000) employed in the Bombay mills were locked out to enforce a further wage cut of 11.5 per cent (in addition to a 20 per cent. cut in 1924) on the pretext of "ruinous" trade depression, not less than half the mills were paying a fairly high rate of dividends. However, the abolition of the Excise Duty removed the last cause of friction between the Indian bourgeoisie and Imperialism. The political effect of this step has been to split the Nationalist movement along the line dividing the big bourgeoisie and the petty bourgeoisie. The life of the Swaraj Party, which stood with one foot in the camp of the big bourgeoisie and another in the petty bourgeois camp, is seriously threatended.

This concession again was not made in deference to the demands of the bourgeois Nationalists. Consideration of Britain's own economic interest was there, beside the subtle policy of politically isolating the petty bourgeois Nationalists by showing the Indian capitalists that their economic growth was not only possible, but even could be promoted within the orbit of Imperialist economy.

In spite of the enormous growth of native production, India still imports nearly 50 per cent of her textile requirements, which until recently used to be supplied by Lancashire. But in the last years things have changed greatly. Japan has been breaking into the Indian market with alarming rapidity. Her share in the Indian trade increased from 0.3 in 1914 to 9.1 per cent. in 1924. In 1925 the proportion was expected to be much greater. England cannot possibly compete with Japanese goods produced by sweated labour.

Indian mills worked by coolie labour can alone do that; and the British bourgeoisie can always participate in the resulting profit by exporting capital to India to be invested in those mills. It is remarkable that before the abolition of the Excise Duty was declared, the President of the Bombay Millowners' Association, N. N. Wadia, visited England and had conferences with Lancashire millowners. In view of the stormy opposition of Lancashire when the duty on cotton goods imported into India was raised from 7.5 per cent. to 11 per cent. without a simultaneous increase in the Excise Duty, the gracious acquiescence of Lancashire in the abolition of the small Excise Duty without touching the comparatively high import duty is remarkable. The explanation of this changed attitude is provided by the following quotation from a statement issued by a joint meeting of the Manchester Chamber of Commerce and Lancashire millowners convened immediately after the announcement abolishing the Excise Duty.

> "If the industrial and general situation in India improves in the way in which it is so much desired, it is clear that the Lancashire industry may hope for better trade as a result. That there is a potential purchasing power in India sufficient to engage the producing power of both Indian and Lancashire industries, cannot be doubted. . . . It is to be hoped that in the new situation now created we may find ourselves moving towards a position where the needs of the Indian market will be met to an increasing extent by her own manufacturers in their class of product, and by Lancashire in the types upon which she will naturally concentrate. Such a state of affairs would satisfy the legitimate aspirations of India, whilst not doing injustice to the Lancashire industry. If this situation frankly recognised by both parties, could lead to the fostering of a better spirit of mutual sympathy, support and accommodation, we would be prepared to accept any difficulties which may be imposed on Lancashire by the present decision in a generous manner." —(The Economist, Dec. 5th, 1925.)

The situation is obvious: Indian and British capital made up their age-long quarrel and came to an agreement against the common foe, Japan. Referring to the abolition of the Excise Duty, the "Economist" (Dec. 5th, 1925) wrote:

> "The fact of the matter is that times have changed. India has now fiscal autonomy, and it is useless for Lancashire to make protests against reductions in Excise Duties or in-

crease in Import Duties. It must not be forgotten that this action of the Indian Government will probably be a more serious matter for Japan than for this country. Lancashire realises more fully than ever that in the future she will have to concentrate her machinery more and more on the finer makes of cloth, and leave the coarser materials to be made by the mills in the East. During the last few years leading authorities have noticed a desire on the part of Indian consumers of cotton cloth to purchase higher quality goods. If this is maintained and extended as there is reason for thinking that it will be, if the purchasing power of the natives is increased, then cotton manufacturers in this country have nothing to fear. It is primarily desirable that a spirit of friendship and goodwill should exist between the people of this country and of India." (p. 939.)

The abolition of the Excise Duty made a tremendous impression in India. Though reluctant to say so openly, the Nationalists generally recognised it as an unmistakable sign of a "change of heart" on the part of Britain; and a "change of heart" was all that the Nationalists wanted as the price for their "wholehearted and honourable co-operation" with the British Government on the basis of the reformed constitution.

Another very significant event was the appointment of a committee to investigate and recommend under what conditions foreign capital should be admitted into India. The report of the committee accepts all the conditions laid down by the minority of the Fiscal Commission. This means that in the immediate future industrialisation of India will be carried on jointly by Indian and British capital.

It will be interesting to examine the considerations which induced British imperialism radically to change its economic policy in India, as a by-product of which change the aspirations of the native bourgeoisie have been to a great extent satisfied. The political consideration has already been mentioned. It is the recognition of the fact that the struggle for national freedom is no longer the political expression of the comparatively weak capitalist and intellectual classes. Its social basis has been enormously widened to include practically the entire population. Its objective programme has, therefore, changed from constitutional agitation for economic concession and administrative reform to —Revolution. The quarrel between imperialism and the native bourgeoisie was over the division of the surplus value produced by the Indian masses. It will pay imperialism to lessen its lion's share to tiger's share, rather than to risk the loss of everything. British imperialism acted according to the Hindu dictum—"Faced with total destruction, the wise forego half."

An examination of the economic consideration will, however, show that it will not cost imperialism nearly as much to buy off the services of the Indian bourgeoisie and even the upper stratum of the middle classes, as against the revolutionary danger coming from the masses. As a matter of fact, it will cost nothing.

The interest of British capitalism demands not only a guarding of the Indian market against Japanese and American aggression; a continual extension of the market is also demanded. Markets must be found—created—for the British manufactures consumed in Central and Eastern Europe before the war. India offers great possibilities in that direction. But the economic ruin of the Central European countries greatly reduced the purchasing power of India because the greater part of Indian export used to be taken by those countries. That means, just at the moment when British capitalism wants a bigger market in India, there is a shrinkage in the Indian market. In spite of a rise in the value of the total foreign trade of India (Rs. 5,890,000,000 in 1923-24), the volume was 28 per cent. less than in 1914. The reason of this shrinkage is this. While on the average 60 per cent. of India's imports come from Britain, about 60 per cent. of her exports go to countries outside the British Empire. Since the war most of the European countries, that used to consume such a large portion of Indian exports, bought much less. The situation is illustrated by the following table:

Total Amount of Exports to:	Rupees 1914	Rupees 1922
Austria and Hungary	99,748,000	8,355,000
Belgium	120,648,000	80,032,000
France	176,827,000	98,270,000
Germany	263,558,000	162,777,000
Italy	78,351,000	58,378,000
Russia	24,542,000	35,000

Germany's share went down to as little as 13,859,000 in 1920.

This serious fall in her export trade naturally reflected upon India's ability to import, ultimately hurting the British manufacturers, since the major part of her import comes from Britain. All along, a large surplus of export over import represented the proceeds of imperialist exploitation, because the major portion of that surplus was absorbed to liquidate "India's obligations in Britain." In 1920 the balance of Indian trade (a balance artificially maintained in the interests of imperialism) was upset. Import showed an enormous (890,000,000) excess over exports. Next year the disparity was reduced to 440,000,000 by a corresponding reduction in imports. The situation was extremely alarming for imperialism. There was a heavy deficit in the Budget. The representative of the Government of India, Charles Innes, informed the Imperial Economic Conference (London, 1923):

> "Thanks to the war and disorganisation caused by the war, we sell less and, therefore, we buy less. This decrease of trade hits us in many ways."

Further on the same speaker explained the new economic policy of the Government of India. He said:

> "I am aware that it has caused some alarm in this country, but if, as we hope, the result of this policy (of protection) is to increase the wealth and productiveness of India, then, those who trade with India have nothing to fear. Already that trade is considerable in volume, but it is small in comparison with the size of the country and the population. In India we have 315 millions of the people—roughly one-fifth of the human race, and if only we can raise the standard of living of these millions and increase their capacity to consume goods, India's potentialities as a factor in international trade and as a market are almost limitless."

In the new state of world economy, it has become impossible for the British capitalists to extract tribute from India in the shape of a large unpaid surplus of export over import. The greater part of the foreign market for Indian produce of raw material has been ruined almost beyond repair. Therefore, imperialist plunder must find a different expression. To arrest the shrinkage of British trade with India, caused by the reduction in the latter's export trade, her purchasing power should be otherwise increased. This can be done by raising the standard of living of the Indian people. The standard of living of the Indian people, again, cannot be raised unless the choking grip on her economic life is considerably loosened. On the other hand, since a sufficient market for Indian raw produce cannot be found abroad, it must be created inside the country. This again must lead to industrialisation. Industrialisation of a country with such enormous resources of raw material, cheap labour and potentially unlimited markets, in its turn will open up for British capital new fields guaranteeing the possibility of almost fabulous accumulation. British capital invested in India will at the same time extend the market for the production of home industries.

These are, then, the fundamental considerations which induced British imperialism to adopt a new colonial policy permitting the growth of Indian capitalism within certain limits.

To sum up, since 1916 the British Government has introduced a series of economic measures that are greatly beneficial to the Indian bourgeoisie. Consequently the antagonism between imperialism and Indian capitalism has been, at least for the time being, almost eliminated. The political result of this changed economic relation has been reflected in a steady decline of the Nationalist demand, and a pitiable bankruptcy of the mainly petty bourgeois Swaraj Party, whose programme reflected purely capitalist interests.

What are the cardinal demands of the Nationalist bourgeoisie? Impetus to the industrialisation of the country; fiscal autonomy; protection. All these have been realised incidentally, in consequence of the attempts of British capitalism to overcome the serious post-war crisis by means of a re-adjustment of the economic basis of the Empire. The demand for self-government was put forward on the hypothesis that unless the native bourgeoisie possessed some political power, the programme of the free development of Indian capitalism could not be realised. Now, it is demonstrated in practice that the economic programme of bourgeois Nationalism can be realised, in spite of the imperialist opposition to a rapid political change demanded by the petty bourgeoisie. In other words, the bourgeoisie have been convinced that their economic development is possible within the framework of imperialism.

PART II

THE POLITICS OF COMPROMISE

CHAPTER VI. THE RISE OF THE SWARAJ PARTY

THE future of Indian politics will be determined by the new economic situation. As a matter of fact, the Nationalist movement during the last five years has been greatly influenced by the changing economic relations between imperialism and the native bourgeoisie. Successive concessions to Indian capitalism have, since 1921, coincided with a steady decline in the Nationalist political demand. This process has caused a regrouping of forces on the basis of a class differentiation inside the Nationalist ranks. This process of class differentiation inside the Nationalist movement reached a climax in the split of the Swaraj Party. For three years the Swaraj Party maintaind a formal relation between the bourgeoisie and the people as a whole by making the interests of native capital the basis of its "national demand." Now that the rapprochement with imperialism is practically complete, the bourgeoisie do not need the superficial political radicalism of the middle class intellectuals. Therefore, the Right Wing of the Swaraj Party, which consciously represents capitalist interests, declares in favour of political peace and breaks away to join the Liberal ranks. The majority of the Swaraj Party, which loudly reiterate their determination to keep up the parliamentary opposition, have gradually tempered their political demands to small measures of administrative reform. Only the question of prestige stands in the way. The Swaraj Party is naturally anxious to save its face, while imperialism demands unconditional surrender.

Eventually, after some oratorical explosions to cover the retreat, the middle class of the Swaraj Party will follow the Right Wing to the camp of a united constitutional bourgeois opposition.* There is no essential difference between "honourable co-operation" and "responsive co-operation," their respective slogans. Both are agreed on principle that co-operation with the British Government is the best practical policy. The question is how soon and on what condition the co-operation will be offered. The split in the Swaraj Party, therefore, is more likely to be between the Right and the Centre as against the petty bourgeois Left than as it appears now, between the Right and the rest of the party.†

The result of this impending split will be the conclusive detachment of the bourgeoisie from the anti-imperialist struggle. Another consequence of the split in the Swaraj Party will be the political unemployment, so to say, of the lower middle class intellectuals and the politically conscious section of the petty bourgeoisie.

---

* Since this was written, in the beginning of 1926, the Swarajist leader Pundit Motilal Nehru signed the pact with the Responsivists declaring in favour of accepting Ministerial office. The Party refused to ratify the pact. Thus the breakaway of the Responsivists became an accomplished fact, and a new schism became noticeable inside the majority.

† The rejection by the All-India Congress Committee meeting at Ahmedabad, on May 5th, 1926, of the Sabarmati Pact in favour of accepting office, indicates that the line of differentiation inside the Swaraj Party does not lie between the Responsivists and the orthodox majority. If the rank and file assert themselves, the bluff of the present orthodox leadership will be called, and before long Motilal Nehru may be found crossing the Rubicon with his retinue.

Ever since the breakdown of the movement of mass passive resistance, thanks to the counter-revolutionary leadership of Gandhi and his followers, the Swaraj Party became the vanguard of the Nationalist movement. A review of its career, therefore, will help us to make a correct estimate of the situation. It will show how bourgeois Nationalism had been steadily declining until it touched the bottom.

The rise of the Swaraj Party in 1923 indicated a move to the Right. Those elements of the National Congress which had all along been opposed to the boycott of reforms and were against committing the Nationalist movement to revolutionary mass action, were the organisers of the Swaraj Party. The programme of the Swaraj Party brought the Nationalist movement back on its bourgeois (and even feudal) basis which had been somewhat lost sight of in the hectic days of 1920-21. The Swaraj Party replaced revolutionary mass action by parliamentary obstruction as the tactics of Nationalist politics.

The founder and leader of the Swaraj Party, Chittaranjan Das, in the beginning sentimentally talked about the down-trodden 98 per cent. of the population and denounced the desire to replace the White bureaucracy by a Brown bureaucracy. It sounded very revolutionary and attracted the petty bourgeois Nationalists, who had been thrown into confusion by the counter-revolutionary political antics of Gandhi, under the flag of the Swaraj Party. The inherent contradiction of the programme of guarding the interests of the exploited 98 per cent. through the instrumentality of Legislatures elected by the exploiting two per cent. of the population, was not noticed in the midst of the excitement.

The programme of the Swaraj Party was to abandon the boycott of the pseudo-parliaments set up by the Reforms, in favour of entering them in order, as the Swarajist leader ostentatiously proclaimed "to give battle to the enemy from closer quarters." The hypocrisy of the whole programme was, however, evident from the beginning to those who were not blinded by clouds of phrases. The Reforms Act had enfranchised hardly 2 per cent. of the population. For the Central Legislature the franchise was still more limited. On the whole, the franchise did not go beyond the landowning classes, upper intellectuals and rich peasantry. It was to these classes that the Swarajist candidates appealed. This being the case, they could not possibly expect to be returned as the champion of the downtrodden exploited, unfranchised 98 per cent. The enfranchised 2 per cent. live and thrive at the expense of the unfranchised 98 per cent. It is worse than Utopia to believe that the propertied classes would vote for candidates who showed the slightest desire to tamper with the right of vested interests. Since the Swaraj Party wanted to secure for its parliamentary candidates the votes of the landowning and capitalist classes, its programme could not possibly contain anything more than the demands of those classes.

The pioneers of the Swaraj Party appeared before the National Congress at Gaya (1922) with the demand for a change in the Nationalist programme. The sudden suspension of all militant activities ordered by Gandhi (with the approval of other Nationalist leaders including the would-be Swarajists) had thrown the National Congress into a state of confusion. The Nationalist movement was in a serious crisis when the Congress met at Gaya.

The deadlock could be broken only by the adoption of a new programme. At that juncture the Communists put forward a programme of revolutionary Nationalism. The principal points of that programme were:

1. Complete National Independence; Separation from the British Empire.
2. Establishment of a Democratic Republic based upon Universal Suffrage.
3. Abolition of Landlordism.
4. Reduction of land rent and indirect taxation; higher incidence of graduated Income Tax.
5. Modernisation of agriculture with State aid.
6. Nationalisation of Public Utilities.
7. Industrialisation of the country with State aid.
8. Eight-hour day and minimum wage.

Had C. R. Das, who was the President of the Gaya Congress, been sincere in his previous pronouncement, that he stood for "Swaraj for the 98 per cent.", such a programme should have enlisted his support. But the programme proposed by the Communists was not even discussed in the Congress, although it was the dominating topic of the press for two weeks. The Nationalist press joined the imperialist papers in denouncing the programme as "Bolshevist."

In that crisis there were two ways before the Nationalist movement—either to break away from the deadening grip of counter-revolutionary pacifism in order to go ahead boldly in the revolutionary path; or to repent the involuntary revolutionary deviation of the preceding two years and return to the good old constitutionalism. The

Swaraj Party appeared on the scene as the pioneer in the second path. Immediately after the inauguration of the Swaraj Party, the Communists, in an open letter to C. R. Das, again pointed out that there was no middle course between revolution and compromise with imperialism. It was also predicted in the same open letter that owing to the existence in its ranks of the mutually exclusive tendencies of compromising constitutionalism and revolutionary Nationalism, the Swaraj Party would split before long.

The Open Letter to C. R. Das concluded as follows:—" But in reality, the Deshbandhu with his revolutionary following again finds himself in the minority, because the majority of the new party (Swaraj), which appears to be formed under his leadership, subscribes much less to the socio-political views of Mr. Das than do the die-hards of the " no-change " cult, who remain in control of the Congress machinery. The result of such a combination can and will be either that Mr. Das will soon have to abandon his original position in favour of " Responsive Co-operation " of the Mahratta Nationalists or that he will have to part company with them in order to organise the third party inside the National Congress—the Party which reflects clearly the interests of the uncompromising revolutionary elements of our society, and which will infuse vigour into the national struggle by means of revolutionary mass action.

" This equivocal position will be cleared by a second split in the Congress camp. To force this inevitable separation of the revolutionary forces from the embrace of the Right Wing, which will bring the Congress back practically under the influence of Liberalism, is the task before you. Only by breaking away from the Right Wing, which in the name of Nationalism has repudiated the tactics of militant non-co-operation, your Party (Swaraj) will stand out as the vanguard of the National Army."

This warning given in February, 1923, proved to be prophetic. Das went back on his own words.

Notwithstanding the sentimental utterances of its founder, the Swaraj Party became the party of the bourgeoisie—the Left Wing of bourgeois Nationalism. This aspect of its character was made clear in its programme and election manifesto. In the programme, Swaraj (self-government) was interpreted as " an effective control of the existing machinery and system of Government and the right to frame a Constitution." It is to be noted that the same people, who but two years ago had rejected the reforms as inadequate, were prepared to accept the " machinery and system of government " set up by the reforms only on the condition that they could have " an effective control " on them. What would be considered " effective control " was open to discussion. Another point in the programme was " to protect private and individual property, and to foster the growth of individual wealth." This should be the cardinal point in the programme of a party that sought the vote of the propertied classes. The attitude of the party toward the landed aristocracy was remarkable. The following was contained in the election manifesto which was an *exposé* of the Party programme.

> " It is to be noted with regret that the tongue of slander has of late been more than usually busy to estrange them (landowners) from the Swaraj Party. The Swarajya which the Party aims at is represented as something which has

> no place whatever for this ancient order, the members of which have in the past furnished many a brilliant chapter to the history of the country, and even in these degenerate days have a number of ardent Nationalists among them. The Party can only appeal to these latter to set at rest the doubts and misgivings of their less enlightened brethren by explaining to them the obvious fact that those who desire to help in the building up of Swarajya cannot possibly dream of such madness as to undermine the very foundations of society as it has existed for hundreds of years in India by trying to eliminate an important and influential class from it. True it is that the Party stands for justice to the tenant, but poor indeed will be the quality of that justice if it involves any injustice to the landlord."

Still more : C. R. Das himself had to repudiate his own irresponsible previous statement as regards the social affiliation of the Swaraj Party, in order to win the confidence of the land-owning classes. In reply to the Secretary of the Behar Panchayet (village union) Association, he wrote :

> "I do not desire any friction between landlords and tenants. I have opposed the idea of such class war from public platforms. The question of the repeal of the Permanent Settlement is an undesirable question to raise and, in my opinion, whatever steps are taken must be taken after the attainment of self-government and, even then, only as a matter of agreement between the landlords and the tenants."

There could not be any doubt about the social

affiliation of the Swaraj Party. By making itself the rather noisy spokesman of interests that had been reconciled to imperialist domination, the Swaraj Party launched upon a life of " bluff and bluster " (to borrow the phrase of a Liberal Nationalist journal) which was bound to be short. The fact that the Swarajists failed to get a majority of the parliamentary seats (on the whole, less than 30 per cent. of the total elected seats in the central and 8 provincial legislatures) shows that the big landlords and the upper strata of the bourgeoisie did not welcome the voluntary services of the new party. Being essentially a somewhat radical expression of bourgeois Nationalism, the Swaraj Party was obliged to moderate its already sufficiently moderate political demand to keep pace with the economic rapprochment between native capitalism and imperialism. Its very social orientation had imposed upon the Swaraj Party the inevitable necessity of this political climb-down.

Chapter VII. The Fiasco of the National Demand

Immediately after entering the Legislative Assembly, the Swaraj Party turned back on the original "National Demand" which was for immediate self-government. The "National Demand" was watered down to win the approbation of the moderate bourgeois parties. The resolution finally moved was :

> "This Assembly recommends to the Governor-General in Council that he be pleased to take at a very early date the necessary steps (including, if necessary, procuring the appointment of a Royal Commission) for revising the Government of India Act so as to secure for India a full self-governing Dominion status within the British Empire and Provincial Autonomy in the Provinces."

There was no "ultimatum" in this resolution as boastingly promised by the Swarajists during the election campaign nearly two months before. In fact, the demand was quite within the sphere of the 1919 Reform, which provides for further advance after a period not exceeding ten years. The original Swarajist programme was to adopt the policy of "uniform, continuous and consistent obstruction to make government through Assembly and Councils impossible," if the Government rejected the Nationalist ultimatum. But in pledging their support to the moderated "National Demand," the Right Nationalist parties stipulated that obstruction should never be launched unless it was agreed to by three-fourths of the combined membership of the Nationalist Party (a parliamentary coalition of the Swarajists and Independents). This agreement meant another long step backwards.

The dissatisfaction with the clumsiness of the administrative machinery set up by the Reforms and the demand for their early readjustment were prevalent among all the three Nationalist parties namely, Liberals, Independents and Swarajists. The latter's attitude differed in that they challenged the preamble of the Government of India Act, which made the British Parliament the judge of the time and manner of India's progress towards self-government. This radicalism, however, was soon abandoned in practice. An amendment was moved by the Swarajist leader to the joint Nationalist resolution. The support of all the elected Nationalist members had been assured for the Amendment which was :

> "That the following be substituted for the original resolution. This Assembly recommends to the Governor-General in Council to take steps to have the Government of India Act revised with a view to establish a full responsible government in India and for the purpose (a) to summon at an early date a representative round table conference to recommend with due regard to the protection of the rights and interests of important minorities the scheme of a constitution for India, and (b) after dissolving the central Legislature to place the said scheme before the newly-elected Indian Legislature for its approval and submit the same to the British Parliament to be embodied in a statute."

This means, the Swaraj Party recognised the British Parliament as the final arbiter as regards India's rights to self-government. Essentially the amendment was more moderate than the resolution. The latter demanded self-government within the Empire; while the former asked for "full responsible government." The reform demanded in the resolution was qualitative: India's political status should be improved from a dependency ruled autocratically to a self-governing Dominion. The amendment, on the contrary, asked for a mere quantitative change: the present partially responsible government to be replaced by "full responsible government." That is, if made fully responsible to the Legislative Assembly, the British Viceroy and British officials could remain as the rulers of the country. What was essentially wanted was that Britain should rule India with the sanction and collaboration of the native bourgeoisie (the Legislature does not represent any other class). Obviously by secret agreement among the Nationalist parties, the more far-reaching resolution was withdrawn in favour of the weaker amendment which was passed by a majority vote.

The debate revealed still more interesting and significant things. The Swarajist leader, Motilal Nehru, who had loudly informed his trusting petty bourgeois followers that the Swaraj Party was entering the reformed councils to "non-co-operate from close quarters—to carry the war inside the enemy's camp," speaking in support of his amendment dramatically declared: "I am not asking for responsible government to be handed over, as it were, tied up in a bundle. We (Swarajists) have come here to offer our co-operation. If the Government will receive this co-operation, they will find that we are their men." He concluded his speech by saying that the offer made by the Nationalists should not be thrown away. "for no good is done by a continuance of the circumstances in which a section of the community is standing outside the Constitution." In other words, the constitution (joint exploitation of the Indian masses by British imperialism and Indian Capitalism) by itself was not objectionable, only it did not make sufficient accommodation for the middle class, which as well as the bourgeoisie declared through the Swaraj Party—'Make a little more room and we will gladly come in.' From the very beginning the Swaraj Party did not challenge imperialism, as it repeatedly trumpeted for the consumption of the revolutionarily inclined petty bourgeoisie. Its plan was to draw the government into a negotiation which might lead to a "gentlemen's agreement."

CHAPTER VIII. C. R. DAS CLIMBS DOWN

THE budget of 1924-25 came before the Legislative Assembly. Contrary to their repeated pledge to throw out the entire budget as a retaliation against the refusal to grant the national demand, the Swaraj Party only availed themselves of the opportunity for a dramatic political demonstration. The Right parties, frankly and consciously representing the big bourgeoisie, would not go very far with their Swarajist allies. As a formal demonstration, the Swarajists contented themselves with rejecting the first four heads of the revenue side of the budget with a slight majority. The bourgeoisie were already disapproving of the futile hysterics of their most energetic spokesmen—tactics which only prejudiced economic agreement and retarded political peace. In moving the rejection, Motilal Nehru again made some significant remarks. He said : "My present motion has nothing to do with the wrecking or destroying policy of the non-co-operators ; and is in effect a perfectly constitutional and legitimate means of drawing attention to the grievances of the country." Mark well, "constitutionally and legitimately drawing attention to grievances," and a few months after demanding immediate self-government as an ultimatum ! Quite good progress ; only in the wrong direction.

The Finance Bill was also thrown out by a still more diminished majority (of 3). But in the course of the debate Motilal Nehru declared that "the Nationalist Party, judging that they have established the principle for which they have contended, think it unnecessary to continue the same procedure with regard to subsequent demands." The great bulk of the budget containing the vital items was voted by the Assembly. Evidently the Nationalist bourgeoisie had called a halt to their wayward champions. The budget was, of course, passed in its entirety by the Council of State, which also had an Indian majority but composed of "sober and practical" men of business and administrative experience.

In the first session of the Assembly the Swaraj Party scored a "series of parliamentary victories" on subsidiary questions. These were trumpeted to serve the purpose of a smoke screen over the continual retreat on vital points of the Nationalist front. In the official annual "Statement on Moral and Material Progress" of 1923-24, such complimentary comments were made on the behaviour of the Swarajists who, only a few months ago, had been looked upon and denounced as irresponsible trouble makers.

> "It is impossible to deny that the course they followed was in form constitutional. . . . In their treatment of the budget as well as in their conduct during other episodes of the session, the Swarajists must be considered to have played the part of an accredited constitutional opposition (p. 281). . . . So far from indulging in the wholesale programme of obstruction and wreckage upon which they had at one time laid stress, they took a prominent part in the ordinary business of the House (p. 281). . . . "It exemplified the growing tendency towards strictly constitutional action on the part of the Swarajists." (p. 287).

An extraordinary session of the Legislative

Assembly convened in May, 1924, to consider the Steel Industry (Protection) Bill, presented an amusing but significant scene. The Swarajists, who have posed as the spokesmen of the "dumb millions" and declared their firm determination to obstruct all government measures, voted for an official legislation taxing the masses to gratify the greed of the Indian steel magnates. No less than 5 Swarajist members, including the leader, Motilal Nehru, and even the stormy petrel, V. J. Patel, accepted seats on the Select Committee to consider the Bill and thus willingly co-operated with the government. Patel brought in two mutually incompatible amendments, one ridiculous, the other going still further than the Bill in the advocacy of native capitalism. The first amendment recommended "nationalisation" of the protected steel industry. Nationalisation of industry before the State was nationalised was simply a ridiculous idea. But the second amendment, in contradistinction to the first, was amazingly business-like. It recommended the application of protection only to those industries having at least two-thirds Indian capital. A clause was added to the government bill embodying the principle of the Patel Amendment and a Committee was appointed to report on conditions to be imposed upon the inflow of foreign capital. The demand for nationalisation was, of course, dismissed without much ado. An amendment stipulating for a minimum wage in return for the advantage accruing from protection, failed to receive Swarajist support.

In August, 1924, the leader of the Swaraj Party, C. R. Das, made a memorable statement to the press. The statement made by him marked a definite stage in the development of the Swarajist programme. He defined the demand of his party as follows:

> "The first step should be autonomy in all the provinces, with some control in the central government, which at present might consist of a mixed British and Indian Council. But there should be some control in the Legislative Assembly, the extent of which could only be discussed at a round table conference. . . . When a pact is concluded, as it must be soon, between Britain and India, defence arrangements would be part of the pact."

The position could not be made clearer. It is to be remarked that "effective control" of the existing administrative machinery demanded in the election manifesto is reduced to "some control;" and the extent even of the "some control" again remains open to negotiation. In making this statement the Swarajist leader acted as the spokesman, not of the entire Nationalist movement, as he pretended, but exclusively of the native bourgeoisie. The significance of this remarkable willingness for compromise on the part of the apparently most irreconcilable wing of the Nationalist ranks, lies in the fact that it was shown immediately after the fondest desire of native capitalism—protection for the Indian industries—had been actually conceded.

In view of this considerable climb-down as regards the essential political demands, the parliamentary fireworks in the subsequent session of the Legislature could not be taken seriously. They were meant to hoodwink the middle class adherents, whom the Swaraj Party was betraying in the interests of native capitalism.

C. R. Das concluded his statement with a declaration of faith and a warning to the Government. He said :

> "I have been a truer friend of constitutional progress and more against the growing tendency towards anarchy than the Government will believe. . . There is a more serious anarchist movement in Bengal than the authorities realised. It is growing increasingly difficult to suppress it. I hope Britain and India will get together presently and come to terms on the lines I have mentioned; for if the Swarajist movement fails, no repression can possibly cope with the anarchy that is sure to raise its head. Violence and disorder will reign supreme. The authorities do not realise that with the failure of the Swarajist movement, the people will lose all faith in any form of constitutional methods. When that happens, what is left to them but violent anarchical revolutionary methods?"

Taking his cue from the British police, the Swarajist leader called the revolutionary Nationalists "anarchists." He recognised that the economic ruin of the lower middle class, particularly petty intellectuals, had created an objective basis for revolutionary Nationalism, or what he was pleased to denounce as anarchism. As against this revolutionary danger he suggested a united front of British imperialism and the Indian bourgeoisie. The latter were no more a friend of "anarchy" (that is, revolutionary Nationalism) than the former. Why not get together? The sooner the better. The Swarajist leader even gave a practical reason to convince the imperialist rulers who sometimes show a woeful lack of commonsense. He argued—if you strengthen our position by making some administrative readjustments, we will still be able to carry the lower middle class and petty intellectual revolutionaries in tow, taking advantage of their political immaturity.

The year 1925 began in an atmosphere surcharged with speculations as regards the possibility of the Swarajists accepting office provided that a few modifications were made in the system of dyarchy.* The question of the Swarajists' acceptance of Ministership arose only in two provinces—Bengal and the Central Provinces—where the Nationalists had a working majority and the Governor, to free the administration from recurring parliamentary crises, prorogued the Legislature *sine die*. The rest of the provinces, as well as the Central Government, were practically not affected by Swarajist obstruction. Consequently, in the beginning of 1925, the centre of Swarajist politics shifted from Delhi to Calcutta.

Towards the end of March, a number of Moslem Swarajists issued a statement to the press giving it to be understood that C. R. Das was willing to form a Ministry in Bengal Province. The Swarajist leader immediately issued a counter-manifesto in which he declared that he was "willing to co-operate with the Government provided that the conditions were honourable." In the course of the manifesto the Swarajist programme was once more specified in these words: "We are determined to secure Swaraj and political equality for India on terms of equality and honourable partnership in the Empire."

---

* A system of government introduced by the Reforms of 1919, under which the Provincial Administration was split into two parts—one in charge of Indian Ministers responsible to the Legislative Council to the extent that their salary is to be voted by the Legislature; the other in charge of Executive Councillors (Indian and English) independent of the Legislature and respnosible only to the Governor.

Das passionately appealed to the European Community in India not to misunderstand or suspect the Swarajists.

Meanwhile, in the beginning of April, 1925, the Tory Secretary of State for India, Birkenhead, made a speech on Indian conditions, sounding the possibility of an agreement. In a statement issued from Patna on April 3rd, in relation to Birkenhead's speech, Das expressed his agreement with the Secretary of State that "freedom would not be reached by violence," and pointed out the vigorous propaganda he had made against "this standing menace to the establishment of Swaraj." He reiterated that the only guarantee against revolution was an agreement with the Swarajists.

In his manifesto, the Swarajist leader admitted that "a favourable atmosphere has been created for further discussion"; but expressed his inability to go further ahead unless the Government met "us more than half-way on the lines suggested by me." What were those lines? "Provincial autonomy with some control in the Central Government which at present might consist of the British Viceroy and a mixed British and Indian Council."

The Nationalist bourgeoisie, whose interests the Swarajists had all along been defending, were also calling a halt. Only in the Central Provinces Legislature the Swarajists commanded an independent majority. The Nationalist majority in the Legislative Assembly and in the Bengal Council was based upon the coalition with the Independents. The coalition was breaking down. In the budget debate the Independents had not always voted with the Swarajists, thus sparing the Government further defeats. The Independent leader, Jinnah, on more than one occasion condemned the Swarajist tactics.

He said: "I repudiate the Swarajist claim that the policy of wrecking has the support of the majority of Indians." It was a very ominous repudiation, since Jinnah's close relation with the financial and industrial magnates of Bombay is common knowledge.

After a rather prolonged secret negotiation between the Swarajist leader, Das, and the Governor of Bengal, Lytton, the former agreed to take the responsibility of forming a Nationalist Ministry on the following conditions:

1. Transfer of all departments of the Provincial Government except police to the charge of Indian Ministers;
2. Dyarchy will be worked on that basis until 1929 (when, at the latest, a further advance towards self-government will be due, according to the Government of India Act, 1919).
3. The Governor will undertake to recommend a further instalment of Provincial Autonomy, if the Swarajists administer the ministries satisfactorily;
4. Release of political prisoners;
5. The terms of agreement are to be finally settled at an all-parties' conference to be called by the Government.

The negotiations being secret, neither the Swarajists nor the Government officials stated the conditions. But these were generally known to be the approximate conditions. Later on, after the death of Das in June, 1925, the Swarajists challenged the truth of the rumours about the negotiations; but the speech of Das made in the Bengal Provincial Conference at Faridpur in the beginning of May does not leave room for any doubt that he had agreed to the above conditions. Judged by the standard of the Faridpur speech, these conditions might be fully acceptable by the Swarajists. Besides, in the midst of the rumpus over the ugly exposure of the secret negotiations, the following admissions were forthcoming from Nehru and Gandhi, both of whom were supposed to be parties to the negotiations.

In an interview to the press (quoted in the editorial of "The Bengalee," July 28th, 1925), Gandhi stated:

> "I did not know that what was going on between Lord Lytton and Deshbandhu (C. R. Das) could be described as negotiations. But some kind of communications were certainly going on betwen Lord Lytton and Desbandhu through an intermediary. I did not know the actual and verifiable content of those communications, but I knew perhaps the general trend which it is neither profitable nor advisable to disclose."

Motilal Nehru, in a letter (quoted in the editorial of the "Bengalee," August 4th), wrote:

> "Deshbandhu did communicate to me from time to time certain proposals which, he said, he had received from Lord Lytton through a friend. . . I shall always be ready and willing to discuss with the authorities the situation in Bengal as well as in the rest of the country with a view to an honourable settlement. Deshbandhu was expecting a further communication from Lord Lytton on the subject, and should His Excellency be pleased to continue the negotiations with me, I shall only be too glad to put myself at his disposal."

Chapter IX. The Faridpur Speech

It is not worth while to go further into this episode. The purpose of showing the rapid decline in the Swarajist demand will best be served by a simple perusal of Das' Faridpur speech. Here there is no secret negotiation to be exposed; no room for denial; no place for doubt. The Faridpur speech was the most official and authoritative statement of the Party's policy. The following are the most characteristic passages of the speech:

> "Then comes the question as to whether this ideal is to be realised within the Empire or outside it. The answer which the Congress has always given is within the Empire, if the Empire will recognise our rights, and outside the Empire if it does not . . . . If the Empire furnishes sufficient scope for the growth and development of our national life, the Empire idea is to be preferred. . .
>
> "Indeed, the Empire gives us a vivid sense of many advantages. Dominion Status to-day is in no sense servitude. It is essentially an alliance by consent of those who form part of the Empire for material advantages in the real spirit of co-operation. Free alliance necessarily carries with it the right of separation. . . . It is realised that under modern conditions no nation can live in isolation and the Dominion Status, while it affords compete protection to each constituent composing the great Commonwealth of Nations called the British Empire, secures to each the right to realise itself, develop itself and fulfil itself, and, therefore, it ex-

presses and implies all the elements of Swaraj which I have mentioned.

"To me the idea is specially attractive because of its deep spiritual significance. I believe in world peace, in the ultimate federation of the world; and I think that the great Commonwealth of Nations called the British Empire—a federation of diverse races, each with its distinct life, distinct civilisation, its distinct mental outlook—if properly led with statesmen at the helm, is bound to make lasting contribution to the great problem that awaits the statesman, the problem of knitting the world ino the greatest federation the mind can conceive, the federation of the human race. . . I think it is for the good of India, for the good of the commonwealth, for the good of the world, that India should strive for freedom within the commonwealth and so serve the cause of humanity."

The idea contained in this quotation hardly needs any commentary. The utterance is inspired by the conviction that India can develop—can have "the opportunity of self-realisation, self-development and self-fulfilment"—as a part of and therefore, under the protection of the British Empire. Mr. Das' love for the Empire might have bewildered many of his trusting followers. But it was not a mere rhetorical extravagance that he indulged in. He spoke with conviction created by facts. Had not India—the India of the bourgeoisie, until now represented by all the Nationalist parties—been accorded ample opportunity for "self-development" within the Empire? Does not the Empire, in addition, hold out to the same India a guarantee against any revolutionary threat to life and property?

These considerations contributed to the crystallisation of the "national idea" as expounded by the Swarajist leader. But to the India on whose bent back this structure of "human unity" will be built —to the down-trodden 98 per cent.—this new ideal of Swaraj will fail to be convincing.

Further, while enunciating the methods by which this new ideal of Swaraj was to be realised, C. R. Das categorically ruled out "armed revolution," and called upon the conference to do the same. He appealed:

> "I ask those young men who are addicted to revolutionary methods, do they think that the people will side with them? When life and property is threatened the inevitable result is that the people who suffer or who think they may suffer recoil from such activities . . . I appeal to the young men of Bengal who may even in their hearts of hearts think in favour of violent methods, to desist from such thought, and I appeal to the Bengal Provincial Conference to declare clearly and unequivocally that in its opinion freedom cannot be achieved by such methods."

The Nationalist movement should shun the path of violent revolution, because that section of the people having something to lose would be against it. Since the methods, without which complete independence cannot be won, are opposed by those having something to risk, the nation must be content with a fake substitute for independence. Still more: a safe and secure corner in the British Empire should be glorified as something superior to National Independence. The people who have lives to live, and property to be profitted by, will recoil from revolution, actuated by the dictum—a bird in the hand is worth two in the bush; but what portion of the Indian population is in that fortuate position? On the authority of Mr. Das himself, only two per cent. Is the life of an average Indian worker, an Indian peasant or a member of the Indian lower middle class worth living? Is the precarious property that the latter two might own worth owning? It is not. Life is a drudgery—an endless misery. Property is a myth. It does not stave off starvation. Volumes can be quoted from the writings of the Nationalists themselves to show that the life of the Indian masses is living death. Those who have nothing to lose are not afraid of revolution. On the contrary, revolution is their creation. So, it is the two per cent. of the Indian population who, according to Mr. Das, will recoil from revolution, because it may endanger their comfortable life and lucrative property; and in the interests and at the behest of this infinitesimal minority, the only salvation of the overwhelming majority should be tabooed as a sinful method unworthy of the spiritual traditions of India. The Swarajist leader had, indeed, travelled a long way in less than three years. Only in 1922 he declared himself in favour of "Swaraj for the masses—for the 98 per cent."

Now, here are the concrete suggestions as regards the conditions for the agreement between imperialism and Nationalism:

> " . . . the Government should guarantee to us the fullest recognition of our right to the establishment of Swaraj within the commonwealth in the near future, and that in the meantime till Swaraj comes, a sure and sufficient foundation is and must necessarily be a matter of negotiation and settlement—settlement not only between the Government and the people as a whole, but also between the differ-

> ent communities not excluding the European and Anglo-Indian communities, as I said in my presidential speech at Gaya.
>
> "I must also add that we on our part should be in a position to give some sort of undertaking that we shall not by word, deed or gesture, encourage the revolutionary propaganda and that we shall make every effort to put an end to such a movement. This undertaking is not needed, for the Bengal Provincial Conference has never identified itself with the revolutionary propaganda. . ."

It should be noticed that what is demanded is not self-government (not even in a diluted form), but " guarantee for the recognition of our right to Swaraj within the British Commonwealth." The establishment even of this Swaraj will be preceded by time and work to lay the sure and sufficient foundation the nature of which, again, will be determined in the negotiation with the British rulers. The Swarajist leader identifies himself with the spokesmen of imperialism by making the settlement of communal differences a condition for the establishment of Swaraj. And lastly, the Nationalist bourgeoisie is unequivocally committed to the programme of counter-revolution. In other words, in case the Indian masses dare to challenge the suitability of the new ideal of freedom to their conditions, the Nationalist bourgeoisie will willingly join hands with British imperialism to put them back in their place. Then repressive laws and discretionary powers against which the Swarajists have fulminated so much, will become perfectly legitimate."

Still one more quotation from the peroration. The entire philosophy of post-protection Nationalism is restated here:

> "I see signs of reconciliation everywhere. The world is tired of conflicts, and I think I see a real desire for construction, for consolidation. I believe that India has a great part to play in the history of the world. She has a message to deliver, and she is anxious to deliver it in the Council Chamber of that great Commonwealth of Nations of which I have spoken. Will British statesmen rise to the occasion? To them I say, you can have peace to-day on terms that are honourable both to you and to us. To the British community in India, I say, you have come with traditions of freedom, and you cannot refuse to co-operate with us in our national struggle, provided we recognise your right to be heard in the final settlement. To the people of Bengal I say . . . fight hard, but fight clean; and when the time for settlement comes, as it is bound to come, enter the peace conference, not in a spirit of arrogance, but with becoming humility, so that it may be said of you that you were greater in your achievement than in adversity."

No apology is needed for these lengthy quotations. Their importance cannot be exaggerated. They are conclusive evidence of the social character of Swarajist politics. The Swaraj Party was the party of bourgeis Nationalism in its days of decline, as the inevitable result of the changed economic relation between British imperialism and the Indian bourgeoisie. Had the programme of the Swaraj Party reflected anything but the interests of Indian capitalism, it would not come down to this nadir of moderation. As it is, it had to readjust itself to the changes in its economic background.

Chapter X. The Evolution of the Swaraj Party

After the sudden death of C. R. Das in June, 1925, the leaders of the Swaraj Party met at his residence in Calcutta and wholly endorsed the "sentiments regarding violence and the strong condemnation thereof laid down in the Faridpur Speech." The Swarajist leaders, at the same time, regretted that Birkenhead's statement of policy had not taken into consideration the olive branch held out by C. R. Das; and consequently the chances of honourable co-operation had become difficult. The Swarajist position had become extremely pitiable. They were eager to co-operate; but imperialism totally ignored their repeated offers.

Notwithstanding the difficulty created by Birkenhead's sabre-rattling speech in the Parliament, Swarajist anxiety to find a basis of co-operation did not flag. The first step was taken by the leader, Motilal Nehru himself, who accepted in July a nominated seat on the Skeen Committee to investigate the possiblility of establishing in India a military academy of the type of Sandhurst. The next move came from a still more unexpected direction. It was the turn of the arch non-co-operator, V. J. Patel, to co-operate with the Government as the President of the Legislative Assembly. The Government spokesman welcomed the new president and promised him full and loyal support of the official benches. On accepting his seat, Patel made a speech which contained the following:

> "I have accepted office with my eyes open, fully realising the implications attached to it. I became a candidate because I thought I could better serve India in this way. The Swarajists

> have been described as destructive critics: our duty is to show that we know also how to construct. The Viceroy has pleaded for co-operation. Sir Frederick Whyte (the retiring President) has pleaded for co-operation. Now I also plead for co-operation. I particularly appeal to the official benches. I am ready in every sense of the term to extend co-operation to them.
>
> "From this moment I cease to be a party man. I belong to all the parties. If the Viceroy wants, I will attend him ten times a day, and my assistance will always be at the disposal of the Government officials."

Thus spoke the leader of the Swarajist Left Wing, all dressed up in wig and robe of office, as president of the Reformed Legislature which but three years ago he had denounced as a trap of the "Satanic" Government. The year before Patel had created a sensation by walking into the Legislative Assembly dressed in Kaddar and Gandhi cap. Verily "they who came to scoff remained to pray."

In September, 1925, the "national demand" was again put forward in the Legislative Assembly meeting in Simla. The occasion was the debate on the Report of the Muddiman Committee (appointed after the first resolution containing the "national demand" had been passed in 1924) to examine the working of the reformed constitution and recommend amendments, if necessary. The committee was divided in its finding. The majority recommended a series of small departmental changes to ease the situation. The minority demanded a Royal Commission to recommend extension of Reforms. The "national demand" was put forward in the shape of a resolution recommending the adoption of the minority report as against the majority report of the Government. In spite of all the parliamentary stage thunder, the second "national demand" resembled the first only in name. In the rather lengthy resolution, the very moderate concrete demand was shrouded with the exuberance of juridical and parliamentary phraseology. Being based on the Minority Report, the resolution essentially demanded the appointment of a Royal Commission. In doing so, the challenge to the Preamble of the Government of India Act of 1919, which makes the British Parliament the judge of when and how measures of self-government will be granted to India—was withdrawn. It was accepted that a Royal Commission appointed by the English Crown with the approval of the British Parliament was the proper judge of the time and measure of self-government to be granted to India. So the paramount authority of the British Parliament was recognised. As a matter of fact, it had already been done in the previous years in the Nehru amendment. This time the recognition of the supremacy of the British parliament was only clearer.

The distinguishing feature of the Nationalist resolution was that it did not demand any immediate change in the constitution. It simply embodied the outlines of a scheme of constitution which should be considered by "a convention, Round-Table Conference, or any other suitable agency," to be called into being by the Viceroy "in consultation with the Legislative Assembly. . . ." It is to be noted that even a Round-Table Conference, which was the cardinal point of the "national demand in 1924" was not insisted upon. A Royal Commission would be equally acceptable. The following are the main features of the scheme of a new constitutional reform recommended by the resolution:

1. Weakening of the power of the British Secretary of State for India in favour of the British Viceroy;
2. Control by the Assembly of the State finances except under the three very important heads of military expenditure, budget of the political and foreign affairs departments, and payment of debts and liabilities in England;
3. Indianisation of the Army;
4. Legislature to be composed of only elected members, but no definite proposition is made about the extension of the franchise;
5. Executive to be responsible to the Legislature in the Provinces as well as in the Centre. In the latter case, the military, political and foreign affairs departments to be excepted for a specified period.
6. Provincial autonomy with some residuary power in the Central Government.

Remarkably enough, self-government is not even mentioned. The gist of the resolution is that complete political peace will be declared if the Government would agree to set up some sort of machinery to prepare a plan of constitutional reform on the basis of the suggestion made in the resolution. It was doubtlessly a reply to Birkenhead, who had asked the Nationalists to produce a constitution which could be seriously considered. The position taken by the Nationalists is very little removed from the position of the Government. The former have gradually brought their demand down to what the latter is prepared to concede. The Government of India Act provides for a further instalment of self-government not later than 1929. It is agreed that on or before 1929 a Royal Commission will be appointed to recommend the grant of a further measure of self-government, having made an investigation into the experience of the first reforms. The latest Nationalist demand is hardly anything more than this.

Imperialism is opposed to any immediate constitutional reform and would not admit any denial of the principle that the British Parliament is the ultimate judge of the manner and progress of Indian constitutional reform. The Nationalist resolution of September, 1925, removed the hitch on both these points. What remained to be done was for the Swarajists to act upon their own resolution. Here they met with difficulty inside their own ranks. The leaders found it difficult to bring their petty bourgeois following around to see that acceptance of office by the Swarajists would be another—a still more effective—form of non-co-operation. This internal difficulty caused a practical split in the party. The Right Wing, represented by the Mahratta Responsivists, openly came out in favour of accepting office following upon the appointment of Tambe as a member of the Central Provinces Executive Council. The bourgeois wing of the Swaraj Party began showing their true colours. They acted logically. Their action was fully justified by the genesis and evolution of the party. The majority leaders, with an eye to the middle class following, still thundered. But a political party cannot be maintained by speeches to the gallery. A split became inevitable when the middle class adherents of the Swaraj Party cesaed to find satisfaction in the inglorious role of camp followers of the bourgeoisie.

The majority condemnation of the Right defection cannot be taken seriously. It was actuated by the anxiety to keep the middle class Left in the party. The latter, whose economic conditions must militate against all compromise in the national struggle, will leave the Swaraj Party as soon as the position taken up by the Right is ratified as the official policy of the party. Without middle class support, the Swaraj Party will cease to be an independent political factor. It will be forced to merge its chequered existence with the outspoken bourgeois party—Independent Nationalists. On the other hand the middle class and petty intellectual elements cannot be perpetually kept inside the party unless the Swarajist programme breaks away from the mooring of bourgeois Nationalism. This can never happen; because socially and historically the programme of the Swaraj Party is the programme of bourgeois Nationalism. By its very nature, the Swaraj Party was a stage of political transition in the Indian Nationalist movement. It is bound to be split in consequence of class differentiation inside the Nationalist ranks.*

The birth of the Swaraj Party indicated the separation of the Nationalist bourgeoisie from the revolutionary masses. The impending split of it is the sign that the big bourgeoisie and the middle classes cannot walk hand in hand any further. They must part company.

Besides, the most recent official action and attitude of the party do not justify the condemnation of Right deviation. Speaking in support of the Nation-

* This forecast, as regards the internal education of the Swaraj Party, made in the beginning of the year has been completely borne out by subsequent facts. The Ahmedabad session of the All-India Congress Committee and the proceedings of the Bengal Provincial Conference (Krishnanagar) were straws indicating which way the wind blows. The rank and file members and the adherents of the Swaraj Party are showing signs of revolt against the policy of compromise with Imperialism—a policy dictated by the interests of the bourgeoisie.

alist amendment to the Government Reforms resolution, the Independent leader, Jinnah, asked the Government:

> "Do you want Pundit Motilal Nehru to go down on his knees before the Viceregal Throne and then only you will appoint a Royal Commission? What has he been doing in the Assembly? Has he not been co-operating? What other evidence do you want to produce that responsible leaders are not offering you co-operation?"

This was obviously a reply to Birkenhead's stipulation that the condition for a further grant of political reform should be full and unreserved co-operation of the responsible Nationalist leaders with the existing system of government. The spokesman of the big bourgeoisie pointed out that the condition had been complied with even by the most radical wing of the constitutional Nationalist movement. This was said of the attitude of the Swarajist leader, Nehru, and, therefore, of the official attitude of the entire party on Sept. 8th, 1925; that is, shortly before the Right leader, Tambe, accepted office in the Central Provinces. Since Jinnah's characterisation of the Swarajists' attitude was not in the least contradicted by the latter, it can be taken as the true picture of the situation. Then there is the following testimony of a very talkative Swarajist who pretends to be extremely radical:

> "The Swaraj Party has really accepted the Liberal Federation Programme to show that the country stood united in its demands"—CHAMAN LAL (Swarajist) in the reform debate.

This damaging testimony was also given before the Right defection began.

Lastly, the following quotation from a Liberal Nationalist organ summarises the Swarajist attitude in a still earlier period:

> "Step by step, stage by stage, they [the Swarajists] have been coming down from the dizzy heights of obstruction to the plainer paths of negation of co-operation, and finally to the acceptance of responsive co-operation as a principle of their political programme."—("The Bengalee" [Liberal Organ], July 22nd, 1925.)

The Swarajists made more progress in the same direction since the above was written. In view of these facts (many more could be added), the official condemnation of the Right defection can be taken only for a bluff which will soon be called.*

Let us look at the picture from the other side. How do the imperialists judge the situation? What is their attitude? Generally there reigns a satisfaction that things are well in hand in India; and suggestions for eventual political reforms to meet the moderate national demand are heard from inspired sources. Here are some examples:

> "Now that India is returning to the paths of patience, it is all important that we should show her that substantial progress can be made through constitutionalism and co-operation." —("The Manchester Guardian," Dec. 21st, 1925.)

"The Near East and India," which is considered to be an authoritative organ of British imperialism, wrote on Nov. 26th, 1926:

> "1929 is not far off, and it is certain that an

* The Sabarmati Pact revealed the hypocrisy of the position taken by Motilal Nehru and his followers.

important step will be taken; if, indeed, it it is not taken earlier."

Commenting upon the appointment of the new Viceroy, the "Times" predicted that the term of office of the new Viceroy would coincide with a period of great constitutional reform.

So, by all indications, it is clear that in the near future, imperialism will make a generous gesture to meet the "national demand" which has been reduced to a harmless limit. This will mark the conclusion of the agreement between imperialism and the Indian bourgeoisie. This may have a still more far-reaching effect. This will enable the essentially bourgeois Swarajist leaders like Nehru, who are still identifying themselves with the petty bourgeois majority, to show their hand, and declare in favour of responsive Co-operation (for all practical purposes, if not in so many words). He would not have much scruple to break the promise of civil disobedience* made at the Cawnpur Congress, and to cross over the line.† In that case, they may even

* Civil disobedience was the culminating point in the programme of Gandhist non-co-operation. It signified mass refusal to obey the laws—suspension of the payment of rents and taxes. Naturally, this measure cannot be dissociated from a revolutionary uprising. It can be put into effect only as the prelude to armed insurrection. When, inspired by this revolutionary programme, the masses rallied round the National Congress, the country was shocked by great strikes and demonstrations in the towns, and gigantic peasant revolts spread like wildfire. Gandhi, in the beginning of 1922, declared that the country was not fit for civil disobedience. He stipulated that no step towards civil disobedience should be taken unless an atmosphere of perfect non-violence had been created in the country. Since, by its very nature, civil disobedience cannot be dissociated from eventual violent conflict with the forces of counter-revolution, the stipulation of Gandhi meant abandoning the programme forever.

† This was written in February, 1926.

take over with them a considerable section of the middle class membership on the plea that there has been a "change of heart" on the part of the bureaucracy.

CHAPTER XI. THE CAWNPUR CONGRESS AND AFTER

THE Fortieth Annual Sessions of the Indian National Congress, which were held in Cawnpur in the last week of December, conclusively abandoned the programme of boycott and delivered itself body and soul to the Swarajist version of constitutional agitation. Under the guidance of the prophet of non-co-operation, Gandhi, the petty bourgeoisie ratified the bankrupt Swarajist programme of parliamentary obstruction. They had nothing better to look up to for leadership than the moribund Swaraj Party, rent asunder by internal contradictions. This is indicative of the pitiable state that Nationalist politics has sunk into under compromising bourgeois leadership.

The following were the principal political decisions of the Cawnpur Congress: (1) To give fullest support to the parliamentarism of the Swaraj Party; (2) to invite other political parties (that is, the parties of the Right), irrespective of beliefs to join the Congress; (3) to support the Commonwealth of India Bill*; (4) to fix the goal of the Nationalist movement at Dominion Status (self-

* The Commonwealth of India Bill drafted by Mrs. Besant containing a project of reform subscribed to by the extreme bourgeois nationalist elements. It proposes some minor readjustment in the present administrative machinery, and recommends a draft constitution for India when she will eventually be raised to the same status of self-government as enjoyed by Canada, Australia, etc. When, a year and a half ago, the Bill was first published, the Swaraj Party refused to subscribe to it. Later on Gandhi publicly declared that he would induce the Swaraj Party to subscribe to the Bill provided that its adoption by the British Parliament was guaranteed. The Swarajist demand formulated by Das at Faridpur almost coincides with the provisions of the Commonwealth of India Bill.

government within the British Empire) ; (5) to call upon the Swarajist members to vacate their parliamentary seats and seek re-election if the Government reject the "national demand" and (6) to change the policy of the Congress as soon as the Government " will make a sincere and magnanimous gesture of good will and good faith."

In the Cawnpur Congress were uttered many oratorical threats that failed to threaten anybody. The Swarajist leader, Motilal Nehru, heroically informed the naive petty bourgeois gathering that if the Government rejected the " national demands" the Swarajists would resign their seats in the Legislatures and begin the preparation for civil disobedience. Remembering that Nehru was a leading member of the Congress Commission which in the revolutionary days of 1922 declared the country unfit for civil disobedience, that threat could not be taken seriously. The demand for the repudiation of the programme of revolutionary mass action, which led to the foundation of the parliamentary Swaraj Party, was based upon that finding of the Civil Disobedience Committee. Therefore, none but a simpleton would believe Motilal Nehru when he flamboyantly talked of civil disobedience after all these historical events. If he found the country unfit for civil disobedience in 1922, when the echo of the great revolutionary demonstration was still lingering in the atmosphere and the horizon was still ablaze with the smouldering flames of peasant revolt, how much easier would it be for Nehru to disregard the pledge, made to dupe his petty bourgeois following, on the pretext that the country was not ready. What Nehru actually promised was that after resigning their seats, the Swarajists would seek re-election on a programme drawn up by the

Congress. Everything depends on that programme. Such a staunch defender of capitalism and landlordism as the Swaraj Party never can and never will seriously consider the project of civil disobedience which cannot be put into effect without the revolutionary action of the worker and peasant masses.

The Swarajist leader himself did not mean anything serious when he made the pledge to the Cawnpur Congress. It was meant for the gallery. He knew that the "national demand" had been brought to such a degree of moderation as almost to guarantee its eventual acceptance by the Government. Civil disobedience will ever remain a hypothetical proposition. Then, we have seen the "national demands" rejected more than once, without evoking any retaliatory measure from the Swarajist side.

As a matter of fact, the Swaraj Party began to climb down from the position it took against the Right dissentients, immediately after the Cawnpur Congress. The leading members of the Right resigned their seats in the Legislatures—Central and Provincial, and declared their intention to seek re-election on their programme of political peace, which they euphemistically call "Responsive Co-operation." This was an extremely clever move on their part. The social composition of the electorate assures their re-election. Nehru and his followers at the head of the Swarajist Majority were outwitted. They immediately made it understood that if the responsivist leaders are re-elected, the party would find it necessary to change its programme, because the re-election of the Right leaders on their programme would show that the country was in favour of that programme. In other words, as soon as the bourgeois voters had made it clear that they have no more use for parliamentary fireworks, the Swaraj

Party would meekly obey and get down to the business of discovering the identity between "Responsive Co-operation" and "Honourable Co-operation."

While running down the responsivist "heresy" —a policy dictated by capitalist interest—the leader of the party paid homage to and received the benediction of the god Capital. On December 3rd, 1925, Motilal Nehru was entertained by the cotton mill owners at a tea party. The president of the Millowners' Association thanked the Swarajist leader for the great services rendered by his party to the premier industry by supporting the abolition of the Excise Duty. Nehru replied:

> "I and my colleagues have done our duty. I assure the millowners that we will act similarly whenever the industry will be in danger of being exploited by foreign or unfair competition. We went in the Legislative Assembly to work for the country, and not for any particular section or party."

So, the Swaraj Party as a party stood solidly as the political instrument of the capitalist and landowning classes, even at the moment it was pandering to the radical illusions of the middle class. The Swaraj Party entered the Legislature "to work for the country"; but it is notorious whom they served. They served exclusively capitalist and landed interests. Now that these same interests (which are identified with the entire country by the bourgeois Nationalists) can be better served by declaring political peace and co-operating with the British Government, the Swaraj Party, as good patriots, will have no compunction to do what should be done "in the interests of the country." The Right Wing leaders had more courage and conviction than the rest. They were the pioneers in the march to the spiritual home. In this period of differentiation between the bourgeoisie and petty bourgeoisie, the Mahratta leaders played the same role as C. R. Das had played in the previous period which was marked by the separation of bourgeois Nationalism from revolutioiary mass action. Just as parliamentary obstruction replaced mass passive resistance, just so will parliamentary obstruction be abandoned in favour of constitutional opposition. A steady change in the economic relation between imperialism and native capitalism, which is the social basis of bourgeois Nationalism, has caused these successive stages of evolution in the political sphere. It was a pre-determined and inevitable process.

This debacle of bourgeois Nationalism, however, does not by any means indicate the end of the anti-imperialist struggle. It only means that the social basis of Nationalism will be shifted from the bourgeoisie to the masses. This process of widening the social basis of Nationalism is parallel to the process of widening the social basis of imperialism by drawing the colonial bourgeoisie economically and politically closer to it. So, the future of Indian politics will be the organisation of all the classes of the native society, except the landlords, the big bourgeoisie and their middle class satellites, in the struggle for national freedom. The programme of the new phase of Nationalism will naturally be entirely different from the programme which up till now has dominted the Nationalist movement.

The formation of the Bourgeois Bloc in the Unity Conference of Bombay forced upon the Swaraj Party the necessity to define its position. It must abandon the ambiguous position taken up at Cawnpur. It must take sides—with the bourgeoisie for the programme of constitutional reform or with the people for revolution. This ultimatum of the bourgeoisie frightened the Swarajist leaders. Immediately after the dramatic walk-out they met the Responsivists at Sabarmati to discuss the conditions for accepting office. The Sabarmati Pact was a negation of the decision of the Cawnpur Congress and the walk-out as a result of those decisions. The pact meant a complete capitulation of the Swaraj Party. It signified the triumph of bourgeois Nationalism and political death of the Swaraj Party. It recorded the victory of Responsive Co-operation which was so demagogically fought at Cawnpur; and Responsive Co-operation means nothing but a complete compromise with imperialism to co-operate with the British Government in response to the concessions made to the Indian bourgeoisie. The Bourgeois Bloc, to which the Swaraj Party would submerge itself through the instrumentality of the Sabarmati Pact, was a *union sacrée* not against the foreign rule, but to fight the revolutionary movement. It would fight the Swaraj Party should the latter still persist in keeping company with the revolutionary wing of the Nationalist movement.

The general elections are a few months ahead. The time set for the extension of reforms coincides with the lifetime of the next legislatures. Therefore, it is absolutely necessary that in the coming elections such candidates should be returned as stand unequivocally on the platform of bourgeois Nationalism. If the Swaraj Party did not fall in line, war would be declared on them. The bourgeoisie succeeded in terrorising the Swarajist leaders who had always stood on the platform of bourgeois Nationalism. But the surrender of the leaders at Sabarmati opened the eyes of the Swarajist ranks. The pact was repudiated. The split in the Nationalist ranks along the class line was complete. The line runs through the Swaraj Party also. Consequently the Swaraj Party has virtually split on the issue of compromise with imperialism versus revolutionary mass struggle for freedom. This is the case in spite of the fact that the revolt in the ranks obliged the Swarajist leaders to go back on their signature to the pact of capitulation.

The Bourgeois Bloc is a historic phenomenon. All the events in the Nationalist movement ever since the betrayal of Bardoli had been heading towards it. The bloc marks the termination of a certain process of evolution. It is the crystallisation of the policy of compromise with imperialism on the basis of the Reform of 1919—to work them for what they are worth and to negotiate for further concessions. This line is dictated by the immediate interests of the native bourgeoisie. On the other hand the compromising elements in the Indian Nationalist movement are strengthened and encouraged by the fact that British imperialism is obliged to meet these elements halfway. The collapse of bourgeois Nationalism is inevitable. It is determined by the economic relation between the Indian bourgeoisie and British imperialism.

PART III

A REAL NATIONALIST MOVEMENT

CHAPTER XII. THE NEW BASIS OF THE NATIONAL STRUGGLE

THE big bourgeoisie is practically eliminated from the struggle for national freedom. The bourgeois bloc of Bombay propose to fight not so much the bureaucracy as any revolutionary tendency in the Nationalist movement. They have declared war even on the harmless stage-thunders of Swarajism. Practically, the bourgeois bloc seeks to make a united front with the imperialist forces of law and order to make the country safe against any possible revolution. The middle class, which still makes the show of a parliamentary fight, is in hopeless political bankruptcy. Economic understanding between British imperialism and Indian capitalism has taken the wind out of the sails of bourgeois Nationalism under which the Swaraj Party has been steering its course. The future of Indian politics (of national liberation) will, therefore, be determined by the social forces which still remain and will always remain antagonistic to Imperialism even in the new era dominated by the "higher ideals of Swaraj within the Empire." These social forces are composed of the workers, peasantry and the petty bourgeoisie (small traders, artisans, employees, students, petty intellectuals, etc.). In the new era of compromise and agreement the economic conditions of these classes will not be essentially improved. On the contrary, they will become worse. The agreement between Indian capitalism and British imperialism is made on the basis of the latter's permitting the former a larger and more direct share in the proceeds of exploitation of the Indian masses. In making this "concession," imperialism has taken all precautions against a substantial reduction of its share.

The share of the Indian bourgeoisie will be increased by a corresponding increase in the surplus value produced by the Indian working masses. In addition to the enormous tribute to imperialism, the burden of contributing to greater and more rapid enrichment of the native bourgeoisie will then also fall upon the bent back of the Indian workers and peasants. The Indian capitalists do not make any secret of this prospect either. They frankly declare that in order to secure "national prosperity"—by which they mean the prosperity of their class—it will be necessary for the people to make sacrifices. While making a strong plea for the protection of Indian industries, the minority of the Fiscal Commission (composed of four leading Indian capitalists and one Nationalist politician) in their Note of Dissent wrote:

> "We recognise that in the efforts to attain a prominent position in the industrial world, India will have to pay a price. The economic well-being of India which we aim at in the tariff policy which we recommend cannot be obtained without making a sacrifice."

Protective tariffs not only increase the price of commodities on which the tax is levied. They cause a corresponding rise in the price of similar articles produced in the country. Besides, a sympathetic rise in prices results all around. This means that in the era of protectionism, the consuming public (majority of the population, will be obliged to contribute towards the enrichment of the small class of capitalists who will derive the profit from the industries developing behind high tariff walls. Industrial prosperity is likely to cause a rise in wages eventually. But the rise in wages will be more than compensated by a greater rise in prices. The real wages, therefore will steadily go down.

The peasantry will be obliged to pay higher prices for agricultural implements, clothing and other manufactured necessities, while, owing to the shrinkage of the foreign market, the prices of agricultural produce will go down. Extension of the Indian market for manufactured articles at the same time will require a prosperous peasantry. Agricultural productivity must be increased in general. Productivity of land cannot be raised unless the present primitive system of cultivation is replaced by modern methods. But the existing land tenure stands in the way of this improvement. Cultivation of land cannot be modernised unless there is a class of peasantry in secure possession of sufficiently large areas of land. This readjustment in landholding will be obviously at the expense of the poor peasantry who are at present tenants-at-will with no proprietary right in the soil. A process of selection will be introduced in agriculture as a result of the industrialisation of the country. More attention will be devoted to the growth of raw materials required by manufacturing industries. This will create the need for large scale farming. Land will be gradually concentrated not as at present in the hands of speculators and moneylenders, who usually leave the cultivator on the soil, but in capitalist farms where the former "independent" cultivators will be reduced to wage slaves. The totality of agricultural production will be raised, the internal market will be extended, by driving the small peasantry off the land—by expropriation. Concentration of land will be caused by the expropriation of the small peasantry.

The artisans will be visited by further destruction of their means of livelihood. If the handicrafts suffered so heavily in competition with machine industry situated thousands of miles away, the destruction will be extremely greater and quicker when the same agency will operate on the spot. The destruction of craft industry will ruin the numerous small traders connected with this industry. Extension of banking facilities, so much demanded by the Indian bourgeoisie, will draw the rural trade more under the grip of urban capital and the small independent trader will be squeezed out of existence in consequence.

The prospect of the lower middle class and the petty intellectuals is not any brighter. They will have to bear the burden of heavy indirect taxation in the shape of higher prices, rents and travelling cost. Nothing is held out to them in return. The promised facilities for technical education will convert a small section of the younger generation into industrial wage-slaves. The problematical Indianisation of the army will only give them the opportunity to pledge the younger generation to the defence of a system that at best will keep them ever on the verge of economic ruin and moral degradation. The petty intellectuals in India are thoroughly proletarianised. They are an overproduced commodity thrown in ever increasing numbers on the glutted market. A proletarianised class can save itself only through a social revolution—by the radical change of the political-economic system that has caused their proletarianisation.

British imperialism has adopted the policy of industrialised India in order to tap the unlimited reserves of labour power. The produce of metropolitan industries no longer enables British capitalism to hold its own in the world market—particularly the markets of the east. To compete successfully with its rivals British capitalism must place cheap goods in the market. This can only be done by harnessing the sources of cheap labour. Therefore, industrialisation of India, which will provide the Indian bourgeoisie the coveted place in the sun, will intensify the exploitation of the Indian proletariat. Unpaid labour being the basis of capitalism, capitalist development of India will cause a great exploitation of the Indian working class. Since the future of British imperialism depends upon its success in profiting by the cheap labour of the Indian proletariat, it will keep the working class to the lowest subsistence level. The entire power of the State will be used for this purpose. The Indian bourgeoisie will be a willing party to the violent exploitation and suppression, because their prosperity also depends on what the workers will produce without getting any return. In short, in the era of "equal partnership" the insatiable greed of British imperialism and Indian capitalism will be satisfied at the expense of the proletariat.

Therefore, the agreement between imperialism and the Indian bourgeoisie does not by any means liquidate the struggle for national independence. Indeed, it pushes the struggle towards more revolutionary forms. The social basis of the Nationalist movement is shifted to the classes which have nothing in common with imperialism—which have nothing to lose but their chains of political slavery and economic exploitation. Class struggle—the struggle between the propertied and expropriated classes—clearly becomes the motive force of Indian politics.

Now arise the questions of organisation and leadership of these forces. Which of the three classes involved will assume the leading role in the fight? What organisational form will the struggle adopt?

Both the leadership and organisational form will naturally be determined by the social character of the movement. The social elements that will henceforth compose the movement for national liberation are the petty intellectuals, artisans, small traders, peasantry and the proletariat. In the existing condition of Indian society, these all belong to the oppressed and exploited class. The movement for national liberation will take place on the basis of the struggle between the exploiting and exploited classes. Henceforth the fight for national freedom in India becomes a class-struggle approximating to the final stage.

Class struggle is not always a struggle between the exploiter and exploited. It is so only in its last stages. In the earlier stages it is not a prelude to the abolition of class ridden society. It simply expresses the antagonism of a rising class to the old dominating class. It simply causes a transformation of property relationship—one class replaces another class as the dominating social factor. In its final stage the nature of the class-struggle entirely changes. It ceases to be the struggle between two forms of property. It becomes the prelude to the abolition of private property and the foundation of the socialist order of society. On the one side of the line stands capitalism as the quintessence of private ownership, and on the other is marshalled the proletarian army which by its very nature does not represent a new form of property. The victory of the latter, therefore, leads to the reorganisation of human society, free from class domination. With the disappearance of property-right, classes disappear.

Although the class struggle in the contemporary Indian society has not arrived at the very last stage, it approximates that stage so much as to have the proletariat at its head. But at the same time the majority of forces involved in the struggle objectively do not stand for the total abolition of property. They are exploited, expropriated; nevertheless, their victory will not be a socialist victory, but a popular democratic victory. So the proletariat is called upon to lead a movement for democratic freedom, which movement, however, will have a preponderating character of class struggle in the last stage. The proletariat will have the hegemony in the struggle for democracy. The objective programme of the proletariat (Socialist Programme) will not be imposed on the movement, but the hegemony of the proletariat will inspire the struggle with the most advanced revolutionary democratic ideals, as distinguished from the hypocritical bourgeois democracy. Democracy is the end in itself for the class which converts the democratic State into an instrument of its domination. From the proletarian point of view it is a means—a step towards Socialism. Therefore, if necessary, as in India, and as has been in Russia, the proletariat should assume the hegemony in the struggle for democratic freedom. Whether the democratic revolution can be quickly transformed into a Socialist Revolution (as in Russia), remains an open question depending upon the class relations in the particular society and on the political maturity of the proletariat. What is conclusive is that on the failure of the bourgeoisie to lead the democratic revolution, the proletariat becomes the leaven of the democratic movement, and will exercise the hegemony in the struggle for democratic freedom. When, as in India, the bourgeoisie betray their historic trust, the movement for democratic freedom becomes a class struggle approximating the last stage. As a matter of fact, the bourgeoisie desert and betray the struggle for democratic freedom whenever the conception of democratic freedom in the least threatens to transgress the narrow confines of capitalist parliamentarism and approximates the freedom of class domination. History is full of examples of such desertion and betrayal. The democratic movement headed by the bourgeoisie is a struggle for power between two classes representing two different forms of property. But a democratic movement which goes on in spite of the betrayal of the bourgeoisie, represents the classes that are essentially exploited and expropriated, although some of them are identified with some form of property. Petty bourgeois property, however, is not a newer and more developed form of property as against the capitalist system. On the contrary, it is a form of property that is bound to be eliminated by the development of capitalist production. Therefore the antagonism between capitalism and petty bourgeois ownership does not belong to that category of class-struggle which is between two forms of property. It is essentially a skirmish on the outskirts of the arena where the final battle will be fought. This being the case, a democratic struggle whose social basis embraces the petty bourgeoisie (including the peasantry) is bound to be under proletarian hegemony. Being essentially linked up with the last stage of the class struggle, it is inevitably influenced by the leader of that struggle. Therefore, the proletariat will have the hegemony in the Indian struggle for national freedom in the coming phase.

The next question is, how will the movement be organised? In what formation should the democratic forces be marched in the battle? To play creditably its political role, the proletariat will, of course, have its own party—the Communist Party. But in that there will be no room for its democratic allies. The party of the proletariat stands under the banner of Socialism. On the way to the ultimate goal, the proletarian party may be required to fight for non-Socialist democratic demands. But it always remains a Socialist (Communist) Party. Its final programme is a Socialist (Communist) programme.

The allies of the proletariat, however, are not just now fighting for Socialism. They, therefore, cannot be in a party which objectively stands for Socialism, though taking part, even leading, non-socialist democratic movements as steps forward. Hence arises the necessity of a party in which the proletariat stand side by side (as a vanguard) with the revolutionary Nationalist elements fighting for democratic freedom. None of the existing Nationalist parties can serve the purpose. The Liberal and the Independent Nationalist parties have never pretended to be anything but the political instrument of the bourgeoisie. Such pretension came from the Swarajists. But the completely capitalist character of the Swaraj Party—as led and constituted at present—has been demonstrated. There are large petty bourgeois elements in that party. These elements, however, can no longer stay in the party which has so completely betrayed the interests of their class. They must either assert themselves to transform the party into a revolutionary democratic party of the people or leave the party. The Swaraj Party does not stand for a democratic revolution, as its programme and record of activities clearly indicate. For all practical purposes it has even abandoned all effective opposition to the foreign bureaucracy. The Party has split under the pressure of class contradictions. The section consciously representing bourgeois interests has broken away. But the party still remains a bourgeois Nationalist party. The social composition of the party—the objective demands of its members and adherents—calls for a programme entirely different from the old programme of the party. The organisational structure of the party must also be changed. A party apparatus adapted only to parliamentary activities cannot be the suitable political organ of the unfranchised masses. Owing to the essentially capitalist nature of its programme, and the limitation of its activities to the narrow parliamentary field, a major portion of the popular democratic forces stood outside the Swaraj Party. The union of these forces with the similar element inside the Swaraj Party will convert the Swaraj Party into a national revolutionary party of the people. The first event in the future of Indian politics will be the crystallisation of such a party.

CHAPTER XIII. THE LABOUR PARTY

FROM several quarters comes the proposition for the organisation of a Labour Party. As a matter of fact, efforts have been made to organise an Indian Labour Party. All these efforts so far have miscarried. On the face of it, the proposition is not the result of a mature study of the situation. Fundamentally, it does not correspond to the Indian conditions.

First of all, the nature of the task should be defined unequivocally. The organisation of a proletarian party is not the question in issue here. The proletariat must have its own party. The analysis of the situation, however, reveals the imperativeness of a political organisation apart from the party of the proletariat. What is needed is not a change in the nomenclature of the proletarian party, but a democratic party which will be the rallying ground for all the revolutionary social elements, including the proletariat. Obviously a Labour Party will not meet the situation. As its name indicates, the Labour Party will be the party only of the working class.

Indeed, a Labour Party will not even be the political party of the Indian proletariat. The conditions for the growth of a Labour Party do not exist in India. A Labour Party on the British model (the advocates of an Indian Labour Party are all in favour of imitating the British model) must have for its basis fairly developed trade unions. These are not to be found in India. So, in India, under the present conditions a Labour Party will be an extraneous growth artificially brought into being. The politics of a Labour Party is the politics of trade unionism and parliamentarism. Indian trade unions are not yet developed enough to give rise to a particular type of political party. Besides, to discharge the political role that devolves upon the Indian proletariat in the immediate future, the scope of their activities should be much wider. A Labour Party of the British model is a parliamentary body. Its programme is to have the grievances of the working class redressed through acts of parliament. Its ultimate object is to capture the State machinery by means of a parliamentary majority. For our present purpose it is not necessary to challenge this programme on its merits. It is sufficient to point out that there cannot be parliamentarism in a country without a parliament. In India the proletariat must take a leading part in the fight for the establishment of democratic government. A form of political organisation that may supposedly be useful for the proletariat in a country with a democratic constitution, cannot be applicable to a country without the rudimentary element of democratic freedom.

The advocates of a Labour Party in India represent the tendency of "Economism." They maintain that the Indian proletariat are still too immature, too unorganised, too uneducated for any political action; that they should let politics alone, organise themselves one hundred per cent. in trade unions, and improve their economic conditions by collective bargaining. This is a totally erroneous point of view. It is an attempt to detach the proletariat from the struggle for national freedom.

To act along this line would not only be harmful to the proletariat, but dangerous to the entire Nationalist movement. As already pointed out, combinations of historic events have imposed upon the

Indian proletariat a very important, indeed decisive, role in the movement for national freedom and democratisation of the country. The fight of the proletariat even for the most elementary, immediate economic demands (wages, hours, conditions of labour, etc.), is closely bound up with the struggle for national and democratic freedom. The basis of imperialism is the economic exploitation of the colonial working class. In proportion as the standard of living of the colonial working class rises, the foundation of imperialism is undermined. The object of colonial domination is to keep the standard of living of the native working class down to such a level as to guarantee a substantial margin of super profit. Therefore, no real improvement in the economic conditions of the Indian proletariat can be realised before the political domination of Britain is overthrown; that is, until national independence is attained and a democratic regime is established. There is antagonism between imperialist interests and the interests of the entire Indian people; but the antagonism between imperialism and the Indian working class (including the peasantry) is irreconcilable. The proceeds of colonial plunder are produced by the labouring classes. The other classes of the native population are oppressed in so far as they are deprived of the major portion of the value produced by the labouring masses. There is a community of interest between the native possessing classes and foreign rulers in that they both benefit (though unequally) by the exploitation of the working class. Thus, while the relation between the native possessing classes and imperialism is that of rivalry, which can be readjusted in a critical moment, the interests of the Indian proletariat and British imperialism are mutually exclusive. The existence and welfare of one depends upon the ruin of the other. The Indian proletariat, therefore, cannot retire from the struggle for national freedom without strengthening its own chains. It must stand in the vanguard of the struggle for democratic national freedom. The first and foremost task of the Indian proletariat is to secure national independence and democratisation of the country. Every act in defence and furtherance of the most elementary economic right of the Indian proletariat is essentially political for it is directed against the foundation of British domination. This being the case, the theory that the Indian working class should organise itself in trade unions on the basis of collective bargaining and in a reformist Labour Party of the British model is erroneous. It is worse; it misleads and betrays the Indian proletariat.

The first attempt for organising a Labour Party in India was made in 1920, simultaneously with the forming of the Trade Union Congress. The Trade Union Congress was not a spontaneous growth. In 1920 the Trade Unions in India were in embryonic forms. They were practically strike committees. The idea of an Indian Trade Union Congress was conceived by a few intellectuals, and supported by the British Labour Party. The latter deputed Colonel Wedgwood and Ben Spoor to canvass the idea of a Labour Party in India. They attended the first Trade Union Congress held in Bombay under the presidency of Lajpat Rai. The desire to promote the projects of the Trade Union Congress and Labour Party was caused by the anxiety of the British Labour imperialists to detach the Indian proletariat from the post-war revolutionary upheaval which had assumed positively alarming proportions in 1919-20. The artificiality of the whole scheme was revealed by the fact that meeting in a period when the whole country was in the midst of a revolutionary turmoil, the Trade Union Congress was presided over by a bourgeois politician with no sympathy for Socialism, attended by a score of Liberal intellectuals of humanitarian inclination, and patronised by the emissaries of Labour imperialism. It was singularly unconnected with the revolutionary Labour movement sweeping the country with a series of political mass strikes. A resolution to send delegates to the Communist International was summarily rejected. The Trade Union Congress did not concern itself with the Nationalist agitation which was in high tide, sweeping the working masses in its whirling course. On the contrary, it submissively listened to its patron saint, Colonel Wedgwood, denounce the non-co-operation movement. Had the Trade Union Congress been the conscious vanguard of the Young India proletariat, it should have plunged into the great revolutionary mass movement in order to snatch its leadership from the faltering and treacherous hand of petty bourgeois pacifists.

Nothing more was heard of the Labour Party until February, 1923, when the Third Trade Union Congress met. By that time the Trade Union Congress had become more unreal—a totally non-working class body existing only in name. Nevertheless, on the agenda of the Congress stood a resolution recommending the formation of a Labour Party. The Congress was presided over by the late C. R. Das, and attended by a strong detachment of Nationalist politicians. It was more of a social gathering than a political meeting. It was well depicted in an article by its Secretary, Chaman Lal, who wrote: "The delegates, an imposing galaxy of respectable ladies and gentlemen, rolled up in rows of luxuriant motor cars." In the midst of that respectable and luxurious gathering, all was forgotten about the unwashed millions. The Nationalist politicians, who dominated the Congress, vetoed the project of a Labour Party.

The project was again revived in the beginning of 1925 when the new acquisition of the Independent Labour Party, Oswald Mosley, visited India. He is reported to have broached the question with several Nationalist politicians closely related to and possessing the confidence of the British Labour Party. In the first week of February, while the Legislative Assembly was in session, a number of Nationalist parliamentarians met at Delhi under the presidency again of Lajpat Rai to discuss the project of forming a Labour Party. The president delivered himself of the following sentiments: that the promoters of the scheme should not be impatient; that they should devote themselves to spade-work—to study facts and figures about the economic life of India; that loose talk about Communism and Internationalism should be discouraged; and that an inopportune pressing of the Labour point of view would help the foreign capitalists. N. M. Joshi, government-nominated Labour member of the Legislative Assembly, declared: "We should prefer an Indian capitalist to a British one." Nothing more practical materialised. The project remained in abeyance. A few months later it was reported in the Press that Lajpat Rai had joined the I.L.P. and was trying to organise an Indian branch of that party. It is not known if the I.L.P. has had more success in India than the Labour Party, except that Sir

Sankeran Nair, an ex-high official, has swelled its thin ranks. Sir Sankeran is a particular pet of the ruling clique of the Labour Party. Attempts were being made to give the seat of the Communist Saklatvala to him in the last elections.

Towards the end of the year (1925) missionaries of British Labourism invaded India with more determination than ever. The crusade was headed by a retired army officer gone Labour, Major Graham Pole. As the president of a railway employees' conference at Tanjore, he outlined the programme of the future Indian Labour Party in the form of advice to the working class. His advice was to support the Commonwealth of India Bill (a scheme of constitutional reform based upon the agreement between British Imperialism and Indian capital) and to demand the right to send workers' representatives to the various legislatures to promote working class interests. Finally, he said: "Labour in India should be careful not to ally itself with Communism. What is being preached in Moscow is anarchy itself, and against such counsels Indian Labour should be warned." The speaker further expressed his intention to form an Indian branch of the Fabian Society.

So, it is clear under what auspices a Labour Party will be born in India, if indeed it ever sees the light of life. The most important aspect of the subject is, however, that in spite of the repeated efforts made by men having influence over Indian politics and fully backed by the British Labour Party, the project does not materialise. There has not been any opposition from the Government. There must, therefore, be fundamental reasons which prevent the rise of a Labour Party in India.

Chapter XIV. Conditions for a Labour Party

Judging from the attempts made, the projected Indian Labour Party will be of the British type. But the contemporary Indian conditions are not similar to the conditions in Britain when the Labour Party was organised. A similar political organisation can only be produced by similar social-economic conditions. The British Labour Party was born in a period of imperialist expansion which caused great industrial and trade prosperity at home. The depression following the defeat of Chartism was broken by trade unionist activities led by an aristocracy of labour, which came into being as a by-product of the prosperity created by colonial plunder. Collective bargaining was the programme of the British Labour movement in that epoch. It was on the basis of that non-revolutionary trade unionism that the British Labour Party was built.

The British Trades Union Congress, which ultimately found its political expression in the Labour Party, proved impenetrable for the socialist ideas propagated by the Social Democratic Federation, the Independent Labour Party, &c. John Burns reproached it for having forgotten how to fight and having made peace, or even having concluded an alliance with capitalism. In a manifesto addressed to the Trades Union Congress in 1884, the Social Democratic Federation wrote: "The trade unions unhappily only thought of improving the social position of the more favoured few affiliated to their body, and they are blind to the misery of the masses. They failed to see that it was not improvement but revolution that was wanted. The raising of wages and shortening of hours, were the loftiest things for which they strove."

In the later 'eighties and 'nineties of the last century, when the theoretical foundation of the future Labour Party was laid, the British Constitution had become fully democratic (bourgeois). The proletariat had obtained the franchise. The Trade Union Acts of the 'seventies were regarded by the labour aristocracy as the charter of social and economic freedom. In such a situation the Fabianism of Sidney Webb naturally proved more captivating than the revolutionary Socialism preached in the earlier periods of fierce competition, enormous accumulation and non-democratic constitution. The theoretical basis of the Labour Party was, that in a democratic society, and in a State which recognised the necessity of Social legislation, there was no need for a revolution; that new political institutions for the defence of the working class interests were not to be created—they were in existence to be used effectively by the working class for systematic social reform. The Fabians maintained that at the close of the nineteenth century Britain possessed a fully democratic State; that the problem was not to secure more political power for the working class, but to persuade the entire working class to make constructive use of the power they already possessed.

The conditions in India are totally different. They are not at all the kind in which the British Labour Party grew, nor are the Fabian theories applicable to them. A democratic constitution and labour legislation, which enabled the British labour aristocracy to divert the proletarian masses from the way of Socialism to that of Reformism, are still to be attained in India. The conditions are rather analogous to the British conditions in the decades preceding and following the passing of the Reform Bill of 1832. They objectively make for Chartism rather than orthodox trade unionism and reformist parliamentarism. Trade unionist politics of focusing the entire energy of the proletariat on immediate economic issues are not suitable in a period when the proletariat must stand at the van of a democratic revolutionary movement. Yet the Indian Trade Union Congress is dominated by that tendency, and a Labour Party which presumably will be based on the Trade Union Congress will unavoidably go the same way. The form of political organisation developed by the proletariat of one country in the period of prosperity and possessing constitutional freedom, cannot be applicable to another country in the earlier stages of capitalist development and deprived of elementary political rights.

Owing to the fact that the objective conditions for a Labour Party do not obtain in India, the tendency of "Economism"—trade unionist politics—does not originate in the ranks of the proletariat. It is an artificial growth, having for its basis on the one hand, the native element of intellectual careerism, and, on the other hand, the machinations of British Labour Imperialism. We have no aristocracy of labour. Indian conditions do not permit the growth of a labour aristocracy. The endeavour to corrupt the Labour movement with the politics of orthodox trade unionism and premature parliamentarianism are made by non-proletarian non-socialist elements. Of late the tendency has even been officially fomented. This indicates how dangerous such politics will be for the Indian Labour movement and for the entire democratic movement for national liberation. Politics of trade unionism and of Parliamentarism (in the absence of Parliament) in India are advocated by non-socialist intellectuals, bourgeois humanitarians, kept (by Government) Labour leaders, and agents of British Labour Imperialism. An Indian Labour Party, granted that it can be organised in spite of the fact that objective conditions are against it, will be controlled by these elements. Therefore, it will never be the party of the Indian proletariat. The Indian Trade Union Congress, which presumably will be the basis of the projected Labour Party, is shaped entirely on the British model, although Indian trade unions are separated from the British unions by a period of half a century. The contemporary social and political position of the Indian proletariat does in no way correspond to that of the British proletariat in the period when the Trades Union Congress was organised in Britain. While the organisers and leaders of the British Trades Union Congress all rose from the ranks of better-paid skilled workers, the promoters of the Indian Trade Union Congress are non-proletarian politicians. Nor are the latter revolutionary Socialists—"professional revolutionaries," the importance of which element in the earlier stages of the proletarian movement has been so much emphasised by Lenin. The present politics of the Indian Trade Union Congress is an imbecile mimicry which might be immensely harmful, if the revolutionary leaders of the proletariat fail to fight it. It is misleading the small section of the proletariat which has been drawn under its influence. In its last annual session, held in Madras, the Trade Union Congress decided that arbitration in the industrial field and representation in the legislative bodies (based upon a franchise embracing less than 2 per cent. of the population), should be the means to defend the economic interests of the proletariat. In the broader political domain it subscribed to the bourgeois Nationalist programme of Self-government within the British Empire. A Labour Party built on such a basis will be the last thing that the contemporary social and political situation in India demands.

It may be argued that a Labour Party in India need not be an epitome of the British Labour Party. It will be a very superficial argument. A Labour Party is a form of political organisation dominated by certain distinct political tendencies. In India it cannot be freed from that tendency without rendering it something other than a Labour Party. This has been proved by the fact that all the attempts so far made for the organisation of a Labour Party in India have tended clearly to copy the British model, and have been inspired by adulterated Fabianism. The above argument will evidently imply that a Labour Party should be organised in India independently of the efforts so far made by elements of opportunism. In that case it will only be a question of name. The (revolutionary) party of the proletariat will be called a Labour Party. Why this nominal variation? Why clothe the revolutionary teachings of Marx and Lenin in the respectable garb of Sydney Webb? With a different name the proletarian party will not be able to accommodate inside it non-proletarian classes, namely, the petty bourgeoisie and the peasantry. Besides, theoretically, a Labour Party cannot be the suitable weapon in the revolutionary fight for democratic freedom. If it is intended to deceive the Public Prosecutor, the trick will not work. As soon as it will act as the party of the proletariat should act, in the given situation, that is, openly take its place in the forefront of the democratic forces fighting under a revolutionary programme (including the overthrow of imperialist domination and establishment of a democratic republic), the name will not save the party, unless it can defend itself by more powerful means. If the Party does not act as the vanguard of the forces of national liberation, it will not be a party of the proletariat in spite of the name.

So, an Indian Labour Party will be, firstly, an artificial creation without vital connection with and not representing the proletarian masses; and secondly, it will be inevitably on the British model which does not suit the Indian conditions. It will be neither here nor there. It will not be the party of the proletariat, nor will it be the common platform for all the democratic social forces. Its very name (not to mention its reformist theories) will alienate the petty bourgeoisie, which must fight under the banner of Nationalism. On the other hand, its trade unionist policies will draw the proletariat further and further from the fight for national freedom.

The task of the Indian proletariat in the immediate future is not to bargain with the imperialist and national bourgeoisie for the removal of immediate economic grievances. It is political, of a very comprehensive nature. It is to rally under the banner of national liberation all the oppressed classes of contemporary Indian society. Undoubtedly the proletariat will fight for their economic demands; but they should not have the illusion that anything substantial can be gained in that sphere without a radical change in the political system. In quest of petty economic reforms the proletariat should not go away from their democratic allies. Yet, this is precisely what the Labour Party will ask the proletariat to do.

Chapter XV. The People's Party and the Proletariat

The people's fight for freedom must be led by the party of the people—a party organisation which will be broad enough for all the forces of national revolution. The proletariat will be in it, but it will not be a proletarian party, nominally or essentially. In this party the proletariat will stand side by side with the petty bourgeois and peasant masses, as the most advanced democratic class. The petty bourgeoisie, disillusioned by the treachery of capitalist Nationalism, are gravitating towards the formation of a revolutionary political organisation to carry the fight for freedom further. But the petty bourgeoisie are incapable of independent political action. Their revolutionary discontent often deviates into the futile channels of conspirative terrorism. The decline of bourgeois Nationalism has given a new impetus to the terrorist organisations. At the same time, the tendency of "going to the masses" is gaining ground among the Nationalist intellectuals of advanced views. This tendency has of late manifested itself in attempts to form revolutionary political organisations, essentially Nationalist, but nominally proletarian or peasant. Naturally, this new orientation towards the working masses is either utopian or very superficial—not based on a thorough grasp of the situation. Nevertheless, it is evident that the petty bourgeois intellectuals are feeling their "way to the masses." They are beginning to understand that the revolutionary fight for national freedom cannot be organised without the active participation of the working masses, and that the latter cannot be rallied under the banner of freedom unless the movement for that freedom is based on a revolutionary democratic programme reflecting the interests of the oppressed classes. This radicalisation of their social outlook will not lead the petty bourgeois intellectuals straight inside the ranks of a proletarian party. Nor is it desirable that the party of the proletariat should be flooded with non-proletarian elements, even though they take on a Socialist or Communist complexion. The radicalisation of the petty bourgeois intellectuals—the search for the way to the masses—indicates differentiation in the ranks of bourgeois Nationalism. The political consequences of this differentiation will be the organisation of a petty bourgeois Nationalist Party with the programme of a fight to the finish against Imperialist domination and of democratic republicanism. The crystallisation of forces in this direction is not only to be noticed in the petty bourgeois ranks of the National Congress, but also in the Left Wing of the Swaraj Party. The consciously bourgeois leaders of the Congress as well as of the Swaraj Party have all along suppressed this revolutionary tendency. For example, in the successive annual sessions of the Congress in the last years, the resolution for the change of the aim of the National Congress from undefined self-government (lately defined as self-government within the British Empire) to complete independence, secured an increasing number of votes. In fact, the majority of the rank and file would have given the resolution a majority, had the leading machinery not been put into motion to suppress it. In 1924, the resolution got a majority in the Subjects Committee; but Gandhi, as the president, ruled out its introduction in the plenary session of the Congress. Many provincial conferences adopted resolutions recommending such a change in the Congress programme; but, to the contrary, the aim of the National Congress was clearly defined as self-government within the British Empire last year, and once more emphasised this year. This has created great dissatisfaction among the rank and file. Even in the Swaraj Party, several important members have publicly condemned the "capitalist outlook of the party," and declared that the "party conspired with the vested interests to betray the people." These markedly revolutionary tendencies are bound to crystallise into a Party of Revolutionary Nationalism in the near future.

The task of the proletariat in this situation is to meet the petty bourgeois Nationalist revolutionaries half-way. Left alone, on their own initiative, the petty bourgeois radical intellectuals will never find their "way to the masses." They are still encumbered with traditional class prejudice which survives economic ruin and political servitude. The very complicated Indian system of land ownership gives the middle classes in several provinces a rather precarious share in the unearned income from land. As far as the lower strata of the middle classes are concerned, this share is an illusion—it does not save them from economic bankruptcy perpetually verging on starvation. Nevertheless, this meagre share in land rent has effectively prevented the petty bourgeoisie as a class from advocating any agrarian reform affecting the system of land ownership. Under such circumstances, the desire of the petty intellectuals "to go to the masses" (Swarajist programme of village reconstruction) will not take them very near to the peasantry, unless they are drawn into the company of a more fundamentally revolutionary class —the proletariat. Since the petty bourgeoisie will not, and cannot, enter a real proletarian party, the proletariat must enter, even take the initiative of organising a broader party. Ever since 1923, the Communists have kept before the country a programme of Revolutionary Nationalism. In spite of the joint efforts of Imperialism and the Nationalist bourgeoisie to condemn this programme as "Bolshevism" and thereby terrify the petty bourgeois Nationalists, the fundamental principles of democracy, republicanism, and agrarian revolution contained in that programme have enlisted numerous adherents. The slogan of a revolutionary peoples' party arouses wide response.

A democratic party of the people with a programme of Revolutionary Nationalism (complete independence, establishment of a republic government, radical agrarian reforms, advanced social legislation, etc.), will bind together all the oppressed classes of contemporary Indian society, namely, the petty bourgeoisie, peasantry, and the proletariat. Under the present conditions, the first two will constitute the overwhelming majority; but the proletariat will act as the conscious vanguard of the democratic army—as the leaven of life of the gigantic mass. In this revolutionary combine of the oppressed classes, the role of the petty bourgeois intellectuals cannot be over-estimated. The proletariat will contribute the revolutionary driving forces; the peasantry will lend their massive weight; and the petty bourgeois intellectuals will bring in knowledge and education. Considering the cultural backwardness—general illiteracy—of the working class, an educated ally will be immensely valuable, provided that the intellectual accomplishments of that ally are devoted to quicken the revolutionary consciousness of the oppressed classes. Linked up with the proletariat in the actual and every-day fight, the petty bourgeois intellectuals will undergo an ever-quickening process of radicalisation. They will demand more democratic freedom in such a revolutionary atmosphere than they would do alone. Pushed by the proletariat, the petty bourgeoisie will also go further towards agrarian revolution, thus drawing the peasant masses into the struggle for democratic national freedom.

For years India has been seething with growing agrarian discontent. But no political expression has been given to this revolutionary factor. A party of agrarian revolution, in the democratic sense, must appear as the organ through which the peasant masses will be actively drawn in the fight for national freedom. Such a Revolutionary Nationalist Party will fight under a programme of agrarian revolution. It will unite the petty bourgeoisie and the peasantry in a democratic struggle under the leadership of the proletariat. It will be a party representing the majority of the people and actively supported by them. It will fight for popular freedom. It will be the Peoples' Party.

The future of Indian politics will be an intensified fight for national liberation with revolutionary democratic ideals, under the standard of a people's party. The proletariat, led by its own party—the Communist Party—will exercise hegemony in this revolutionary struggle for democratic national freedom.